Sick of Me

FROM TRANSPARENCY TO TRANSFORMATION

Whitney Capps

B&H
PUBLISHING GROUP

NASHVILLE, TENNESSEE

978-1-4627-9288-7

Published by B&H Publishing Group
Nashville, Tennessee

Dewey Decimal Classification: 248.84
Subject Heading: SELF-IMPROVEMENT \ CHRISTIAN LIFE \
DISCIPLESHIP

Cover design by Matt Lehman.
Cover photo © Kristen Curette Hines / Stocksy.
Author photo © Lindsey Plevyak.

1 2 3 4 5 6 7 • 23 22 21 20 19

To J. N. Posey whose love of words lives on.
And to H. T. Henderson whose life preaches still.

Acknowledgments

First, to my husband, Chad. You are the best gift I've ever been given. You have always been my protector in every way. You saved me from myself more times than I can count. You said "no" when everyone else wanted me to say "yes." So when you said "yes," I believed you, and for the first time believed that God might actually use me to write a book. You let me dream crazy dreams and then figure out a way to make them happen. You have never, ever complained that this was God's call for my life and yours. You have led faithfully. You serve without fail. And you never let me quit. I love you more than words.

To my four boys, Cooper, Dylan, Ryder, and Tate. Your grace to your limping-along, less-than mom is staggering. Thank you for never making me feel guilty when I say "yes" to God. I pray that the Lord multiplies my prayers, efforts, and ministry to you. You are my most favorite assignment. I will love you forever and like you for always.

Mom and Dad, there aren't words. Your investment, support, and belief in me is indescribable and incalculable. You are Jesus with skin on. I know what sacrifice for the kingdom looks like because of both of you. Dad, it's an honor to be your girl. Mom, thanks for setting the bar so high. Love you more.

Mimi and Papa, thank you for loving me by loving the boys when I couldn't be there. You gave me your best gift first in Chad, and now you are helping shape our boys into men just like him. I'm so, so grateful. Brad and Meradith, thanks for making me laugh and keeping me sane. You are treasures.

Evan Posey, thanks for being my theological review and my first, best friend. Being your sister is one of my favorite titles. And Leslie-Ann Posey, thanks for saying "yes" to Ev and our family. You are perfect in every way.

To Krista Williams, you are the gift I didn't deserve and the one that I couldn't live or do ministry without. Your wisdom has changed and saved me more times than I can count. I honestly, honestly can't believe that my mentor is one of my best friends. Thelma and Louise, forever.

To Lysa TerKeurst, it's not hyperbole to say I'm in ministry because of you. Thanks for believing in me and never, ever letting me quit (even when I wanted to). Thanks for letting me watch you do ministry for over a decade. It is one of the greatest privileges of my life.

To my ministry girls. Emily Vogeltanz, in my life, you're not the fine print. Your impact deserves to be in big, bold letters. Thanks for being my person and always making me look more like Jesus because I've been with you. Lindsey Smith, you're the friend my heart needed long before I knew it, and yet you were right on time. I love your heart and your mind. Nicki Koziarz, you've made me wiser and better. I'm so grateful that you let me be your friend. Wendy Blight, Leah DiPascal, and Wendy Pope, thanks for praying me through. I love y'all so much.

To the girls who loved me for me, Kristen Lynch, Ashley Atkins, Sarah Ferguson, Lori Cher, Christina Sabo, Kelly Hensley, and Monica Blackstock. Too much to say, too much to be grateful for. Y'all mean the world.

To my small group girls, Joyce DeJong, Kelsey Hays, Nicole Huff, Dana Jackson, Evie Kellett, and Cassie Singleton. Thanks for giving me your Thursday nights. It's truly life-giving. I'm better because of each of you. And this book wouldn't exist without your prayers.

To my Crosspointe family, you grew me up and sent me off. Thanks for letting me test-drive all my stuff on you. You are the best people around, and you make the bride look beautiful. Betty Matthews, you held my hand the whole way, and I'm so grateful.

To all my Proverbs 31 team, what a privilege to do ministry with each of you. Thanks for representing Jesus so well.

And to B&H and LifeWay, thanks for taking a chance on this girl. I'm still quite shocked and yet, tearfully glad.

Contents

Sick of Me

I'm sick of me."

I went to lunch with a girlfriend not long ago, and that's what I said. And I meant it. I'm so, so tired of thinking about me. I'd like to tell you that I'm not *that* self-absorbed, but the truth is, I am. And I'm sick of it.

A lot of it is superficial and temporal. What do people think of me? Why does she have friends and invitations I don't? Why can't I lose the squishiness that makes my favorite jeans feel like they are literally squeezing the life right out of me? What's so wrong with me that other women can create change or peace or joy or the perfect Pinterest-worthy life, but I can't? All of that surface stuff is there.

But honestly, more than some of my "me" preoccupation is spiritual. I'm tired of thinking about "my purpose." I'm worn out trying to live like "who I am in Christ." I'm exhausted by the endless pursuit to be "the best version of me," but stuck with the very ordinary, still struggling version of me. And when I double down my efforts and strive to be better than I am, live my best life and change, I'm met with books and sermons that deal with more "me-ness."

I am a victorious, daughter of the most High God, called to let go of her crippling anxiety and perfectionism. A woman who ought to live loved and accepted and whole.

These are good (some of them brilliant) lessons that are beneficial. They just aren't helping *me*. What is wrong with me? And there it is again. Me. Her. Self. And that's part of my problem, even my good, Bible-study girl intentions and efforts are kind of all about me. What did I get out of it? What is my takeaway? What does this passage say about me?

What I've been doing isn't working. I want to grow spiritually; in fact, I think I'm desperate to. I buy the books, do the Bible studies, listen to all the podcasts, and strive for biblical community; but it's just not making a difference. I'm trying. I really, really am.

And I bet you are too. I've met you. I've talked with you. I suspect your reading list looks like mine. I imagine you've tried all the same stuff I have. I imagine we read similar devotions, use some of the same apps, pin the same images, and share the same quotes. I suspect our friendships are made of similar stuff.

Now maybe you aren't sick of you, or perhaps you wouldn't put it that way. Maybe you're just discouraged. Or, do you wonder why your life doesn't feel easy and light? Perhaps you've sensed, like me that despite all your spiritual striving, something feels off in a way you can't quite describe. I get it. I really do. And I get the frustration. The inability to put into words what's wrong.

(Something isn't right, but I'm not sure what.)

If I had to sum it up, I'd say this. For all our best efforts, we don't look dramatically more like Jesus today than we did yesterday. We aren't growing more spiritually mature. We may know a bit more, but our lives don't bear the difference. I have countless lists and tips for better marriages, friendships, and finances. But do I really, truly look more like Jesus?

No.

That day at lunch my friend reached across the table and said, "Then stop telling me about you. Tell me about Jesus."

Her words gutted me in the best possible way. Do you know that feeling? The sucker punch that takes your breath away, and kind of makes you want to puke? I usually get it when I'm listening to a sermon that I'm sure is for "everybody else" and then my pastor says something that is clearly—too clearly—meant for me. That's what her words felt like. I thought we were just having a nice, honest conversation, and she had to go and say something like that. And yet that one comment struck me in a way that awakened something soulful and sincere in me.

She was right, and it hurt. But she wasn't finished.

"Whit, you are the most sincere, real person I know. You are self-aware and transparent, maybe to a fault. Your problem isn't that you don't know or own what's broken about you. The problem is you don't seem to really want to do anything about it. It's like you think 'owning' it is enough."

And there it was.

Now if you are anything like me, the concept of "brokenness" may feel kind of played out. A cliché word Christian girls share like Starbucks selfies. We talk about it a lot in church circles. We toss it around with other Christiany buzzwords like *authenticity*, *transparency*, *raw*, and *real*. These virtues are added to ideals like "community" and "fellowship" to form a kind of modern petri dish for spiritual maturity.

If you get all of these elements together in one person or place, you've got yourself a greenhouse for spiritual growth. But what if, *what if*, talking about it isn't the same thing as actually doing it? And what if posting or sharing it doesn't actually change us? What if our greenhouses are just filled with gas?

3

My crazy-wise friend had summed me up just right. I was content to be broken, but not so concerned with being better. I can do transparent. Transformation? Not so much. My mind was spinning. I was thinking of a hundred ways to justify myself, offer up an excuse, or grab a Scripture that I could slap on this situation (likely out of context, because that usually happens when we try to use Scripture to suit us) that would make me sound spiritual. But when I looked at her face, I sensed that this conversation didn't need more conversation. I didn't need to talk my way out of this one. I needed to sit with that truth, and, to the best of my ability, get out of my own way and let truth work me over.

> But what if, *what if,* talking about it isn't the same thing as actually doing it?

The result is what you hold in your hands.

Now to be completely transparent, because how could I *not be*: we can't totally diagnose what's wrong without considering ourselves just a little bit. A woman can't totally ignore her own habits, motivations, desires, or behaviors if she truly desires to change those things. But I hope you'll navigate this dangerous path with me. There are deadly traps ahead. Yes, transparency and brokenness are necessary for the believer. We *do* need to be honest with ourselves about our sin. But we can't, we must not, get stuck there. It's not that transparency is bad. It's that we often get stuck there and don't move forward to the whole point of confessing our brokenness in the first place—*change*. It sounds wild, but transparency really can be the trap that keeps us from getting to the gospel-centered goal of transformation.

We may think it starts with us, but, praise His Matchless Name, it was never meant to end with us.

What We Won't Admit

You know when you buy or download a movie, there is often a feature where you can watch the film and hear the director's commentary over the movie dialogue? Well, my life has one of those. And if you could hear the director's cut swirling in my mind, you'd realize it is composed mostly of *Friends* lines and random song lyrics.

Today's accompaniment is the line from *The Sound of Music*, "Let's start at the very beginning, a very good place to start." I was humming it as I was wrestling with my friend's

> Transparency can be a trap that keeps us from getting to the gospel-centered goal of transformation.

comment. The next line of the song is, "When you read you begin with ABC. When you sing you begin with Do, Re, Mi."[1] (There it is again. Me. Or in this case "mi.")

I think we should start at the very beginning. So I started asking myself, "Why am I sick of me?"

The answer that kept coming to me was, "I'm sick of me because *it's just not working.*"

But *what's* not working in my spiritual life? I needed to get specific. Here's the thing: we can't address what we won't admit. And we only make general progress when we pursue general solutions to fix general problems. Let me give you an example. I'm a little squishier than I'd like to be. So every year I make a

5

New Year's resolution to lose weight. But that's a generic solution
to a generic problem. Really, what does "squishier" even mean?
This year I took the time to identify that the specific thing that
was killing me (and my waistline) was my commitment to sweet
things and regular soda. So I seriously cut back on them. I also
resolved to run a 5K by March. For the first time in my life, I'm
actually making progress, *real* progress, toward getting healthy.
Specific problem. Specific solution. Specific progress in one area.

This is not new thinking. Steven Covey in his book *7 Habits
of Highly Effective People* famously identified healthy goals as
those that are S.M.A.R.T. According to Covey, successful goal
achievement starts with goals that are specific, measurable,
attainable, realistic, and time-bound, hence the acronym
SMART. This advice isn't just good for the professional business person; it's good advice

> We can't address
> what we won't admit.

for the committed Christian, too. And for far too long, I've been
a fairly half-hearted Christian.

So what isn't working? What is my problem? Honestly, it's
that I don't feel like I'm making progress. So then I had to ask,
"Progress toward what?" (Listen, I feel like I should beg you to
hang with me. This seems kind of tedious, right? But I promise
this is the process of getting where we really want to go. And for
far too long I suspect we have rushed past this part—the part
where we truly diagnose what's dysfunctional in our spiritual
lives. So don't bail on me. We're headed somewhere!)

When I think about my spiritual life, what is the endgame?
The same question goes to you: What do you want out of your

spiritual life? Have you ever asked yourself that question? *Why are we even doing this?*

Stop and think about that. It's cool. I'll wait. (Need some prompts? I usually do . . .)

- Why do you study God's Word?
- Why do you drag yourself (and perhaps your household) out of bed and out the door to church?
- Why do you want friendships or a community that affirm and build your faith?
- If heaven is our sure and secure destination, why stress about what our life looks like here?

These are fair, and I'd argue important, questions for each of us to answer honestly and then rightly. For me, the honest answer isn't necessarily the right answer. And I think that's at least part of my problem.

You see, I can answer these questions in a good, church-girl, Sunday school way. You probably can too. I know what sounds right. But while I know the right answer, it's not the honest answer.

The honest answer is that I've spent most of my Christian life *doing* the right things so that other people will *think* the right thing about me. If I do this, you'll think that. If I show up at church and raise my hands at the right time, open my Bible to the right page (without too much lag time between the searching and the finding), if I serve and smile and have good Christian friends, you'll think I'm a good Christian.

7

Sick of Me

While it's hardly comforting to be in the company of the Pharisees, I see myself in lots of the places they pop up in Scripture. Same song. Different verse. Same sin. Different generation.

When I read the New Testament, I can shake my head in disbelief and judgment at the Pharisees' arrogance. Their hubris never ceases to amaze. But those questions we answered earlier, the realization that I do the right things for all the wrong reasons, that I care too much what others think about my spiritual maturity. Hello, my name is "Pharisee."

Countless New Testament passages prove how Jesus frustrated the Pharisees and teachers of the law. Rarely did they come to Jesus to clarify truth or discern wisdom. Their primary goals were to maintain their control and image, limit Jesus' influence, and maintain the status quo.

For years the Jewish religious leaders had curated a system of rituals that let them appear holy without being holy. It's much easier to act holy than to be holy.

The Pharisees had stepped outside of their authority. God alone defines what is holy; He gave the Law to Moses. Its purpose wasn't to be a weapon against God's people, but an invitation to enter into relationship with Him. Over time the Law revealed that none of us can attain inward purity when sin is not addressed.

Jesus came to address this sin issue—for the Pharisees, for you, and for me. Were the Pharisees hands unclean? Sure. But no amount of washing before a meal, in between each course, and at bedtime would make them clean enough to stand before a holy God.

That's what Jesus was saying in Matthew 15:8–9: "These people honor me with their lips, but their hearts are far from me. They worship me in vain; their teachings are merely human rules."

Because they missed the point of the law, they wrongly concluded that if they did enough good they could earn God's kindness. Jesus was clarifying that pleasing God isn't about ritual or performance; pleasing God is about obedience motivated by love and faith. He desires deep devotion, not shallow spirituality.

Now the Pharisees were deeply devoted, but their devotion was rooted in looking like they were without sin or guilt. Public opinion and control were their gods. They were devoted to the appearance of righteousness—to their reputation. I can be guilty of the same. How about you?

Like me, do you sometimes care if people see you doing spiritual things? Do we confess and turn from sins that people can see, all the while ignoring attitudes or actions that are still offensive to God but more easily hidden? Do we say the right thing with our lips while living the wrong things with our lives behind closed doors?

This may not be true of you, but it is all too true for me.

And that is kind of where it went off the rails, y'all. The Christian life is never meant to make people think more or better of me. The goal is for me to look more like Christ, and, should people happen to notice me in the process, for them to think more of Jesus. Can my life display the goodness, majesty, grace, righteousness, supremacy, and sweetness of Jesus? Sure. But it should all rest on and resolve with *Jesus*. Not me.

But that's not on many T-shirts or bookshelves. Instead, we are encouraged to "live your best life" or "you do you." In my best version of me, I decide what life ought to look like. But actually, what frames my best hopes and dreams for my life are my friends' opinions and expectations, television, culture, and of course social media. What I want, what I'm striving for, can be kind of hard to explain or define. Is that true for you?

I've found I can usually pinpoint my unmet expectations by looking at my very real frustrations. Life's disappointments usually expose us to our heart's expectations. It's hard to be disappointed by something we weren't hoping for. Expectations aren't bad. Hopes don't have to go unrealized. Expectation and hope can be the best kind of motivators. But when our expectations aren't anchored in the eternal or informed by Scripture, we end up running after things that are fleeting and ever-changing. Self-infused desires and the pursuit of the approval of others is like chasing the wind, ever-changing, difficult to pin down, and impossible to catch.

Our best lives can't be defined by social media or the culture at large. Our best life can't even be completely based on what we want or think we need. Friend, those pursuits are called group therapy or self-help. What we are called to is *sanctification.*

Sanctification is the progressive work of becoming more like Christ. It addresses the internal quality of our spiritual maturity and is evidenced in external actions. Sanctification then is only applicable for believers.

If we want to define it, we could say that sanctification is both a divine *process* and a human *pursuit.* It is something that the Holy Spirit does in and through us to make us become more like Christ—that's *God's process* in us. But at the same time, we also cooperate with His promptings to become more like Christ through obedience—that's *our pursuit.* This is what Paul is describing in 2 Corinthians 3:18 when he says we "are being transformed into [Christ's] image with ever-increasing glory, which comes from the Lord, who is the Spirit."

I'm a daddy's girl through and through. My dad is the most gentle, thoughtful, loving man. His tenderness of heart and strength of character are unquestionable. He helped me fall in love with Jesus with my heart and mind and modeled what it means to love God and others every day of my life. My life's ambition is to be more like him.

Now I'm fully aware that many (maybe most) people didn't have the joy of a dad like mine. If that's true for you, friend, I'm so, so sorry. Really. That's not fair, and you deserved better. But no matter your experience with your earthly father, our heavenly Father is infinitely more faithful, dependable, kind, loving, tender, gracious, and trustworthy. All of His children should say every day, "I want to be more like my Dad." And *that* is sanctification. Daily becoming more like Him. We want to be more like our Abba, our heavenly Father. (Abba is the Aramaic term of affection that means "Dad".)

This pursuit is totally different than "striking out on my own," "making it up as I go," or trying to be the "best version of me." These pursuits are a bit undefined, self-motivated, and arbitrary. But becoming more like Christ? That's a laser-focused goal with a bar that is clearly defined and exemplified in Scripture. And it has nothing to do with "self," except where "self" is crucified.

Why does this matter? Because I think my spiritual growth (and perhaps yours as well) stalled out because I traded sanctification for self-help. I didn't mean to, and I bet you didn't either. But it happened nonetheless. But friend, as I said, we can't change what we don't own. So, let's compare a life that pursues "our best life" instead of the Christ-life. Consider these differences:

> Self-help depends on my efforts to get where I need to go.
>
> Sanctification asks God to do what only He can, and then equips me to do what I can in response.

> Self-help focuses on my definition of healthy, helpful, good, and wise.
>
> Sanctification allows Scripture to define the virtues I ought to pursue and display.

> Self-help believes that my life is my own.
>
> Sanctification says that my life is God's, and He determines my purpose and path.

> Self-help asserts that knowing my worth and value gives my life meaning.
>
> Sanctification moves me to find my worth in what Jesus paid for me.

> Self-help pursues good things.
>
> Sanctification chases God things.

> Self-help strives to make my life easier.
>
> Sanctification is submitting to a life that may be harder but better.

Self-help has me at the center.

Sanctification has God at the center.

Self-help's endgame is my happiness.

Sanctification's goal is my holiness.

These distinctions may seem like semantics or subtle shifts. But it's in the subtle shifts that sanctification takes place. And the shift means the difference between frustration or fruit. The shift is the gap that separates being sick of me versus being filled with Jesus.

Happiness over Holiness

I don't like extremes. I'm quite comfortable in the gray parts of life.

When Chad and I got married, we had been out of college, working, and living at home with our parents for a year. When the "two became one," so did our checking accounts and bills. I'll never forget getting a call from Chad one day when I was at work. When I picked up the phone, he said, "Hey, do you have your checkbook nearby?"

"Yes," I replied. He said, "I need you to write down and add .07, interest earned."

I was in shock. First, I had no idea a checking account could actually earn interest. Secondly, what kind of person actually tracks that kind of transaction? (Now for those of you under the age of thirty, back in the dark ages before online banking and apps were ubiquitous, we had to track our credits and debits in a charge book. On this log, we would write down check numbers, amounts, our deposits and expenditures. It was the only way to know how much money was available in our accounts. Archaic, I know.)

Anyway, before I met and married Chad, I would balance my checkbook within four or five dollars. True story. It didn't really matter to me if I was to the good or the bad. Close was close enough. (For those of you who, like Chad, track every receipt and entry, I am reformed, *mostly*.) But the gray parts of life never bothered me. I'm not a gal who needs exact precision. I can live in the messy middle.

It's doable (though not advisable) in the world of finance. It's impossible when we think about who rules our heart. Some of us may have read the last chapter and thought, *Life isn't meant to be lived in that kind of extreme. Can't I be governed by Scripture AND ruled by what other people think? Can't I want my life to be all about me AND all about Christ?* (I'd like to think so, says the girl who likes gray.)

Unfortunately, the answer is no. We will eventually give up one in favor of the other. We simply can't give all our loyalty and energy and pursuits to more than one party (Matt. 6:24; 1 Kings 18:21).

One of the most well-known and beloved passages of the New Testament is Hebrews 11. Often called the Hall of Faith, it celebrates various individuals' trust in God. It's a joy to read. But there's a chapter in the Old Testament that is the exact opposite of that. Rather than a "Hall of Faith," it's a "Hall of Failure." Rather than a joy, it's a sober warning. And quite frankly, it's hard to read.

In 1 Kings 16, the Bible records the death, betrayal, and deposing of four kings of Israel. And the chapter is particularly hard to read, not just because of the constant name changes and power struggle, but because of the shocking, sin-saturated conflict.

Why does the Bible record this kind of brutal and escalating violence, evil, and apostasy? (Apostasy is a falling away or abandonment of a faith once affirmed.) Well most importantly, the decline of the kings fulfills the prophetic promise the Lord made to Israel when they asked for a king. In 1 Samuel 8:6–20, the Lord describes Israel's rejection of Him as their king. When God set Israel free from the oppression of the Egyptians, He became their king. They were a theocracy.

But generations later, Israel wanted to be like everyone else. They wanted human kings they could see and follow. God says that Israel has rejected Him, but He will give them what they are asking for. Then God paints a vivid picture of how an earthly king will treat the people, and it's not a good forecast. First and 2 Kings are the fulfillment of all God described. God knew all of this was coming. He told Israel that their kings would turn from Him and turn on them.

Even though the Bible teaches that this failure is coming, it's still shocking to read about the kings' selfishness and idolatry, and the sorrowful consequences that they brought upon themselves and their people. Amidst its darkness, if a story of the kings and Israel teaches us anything, it's that when our hearts turn from God, they always turn toward self. This isn't a place for gray. There is no in-between. This is black and white.

Rather than trust God, we trust ourselves. Instead of pleading for forgiveness, we strategize how to get our way or fix things ourselves. If God is not in charge, we will scheme solutions to the problems that our selfishness created.

Just look at this summary:

- Elah is king for two years before Zimri kills him.
- Zimri reigns for seven days until Israel turns on him, naming Omri as king.

- Zimri commits suicide rather than face Omri's army.
- Tibni, whom half the country chose as king, died in a civil war with Omri.
- Ahab, Omri's son, succeeds him as king, but because of his sin and God's judgment, both of his sons die.

That's the historical summary. There's a sin summary that's even more telling. Idolatry. Betrayal. Murder. Jealousy. Selfish ambition. Those are just the obvious ones. I can assure you there were more. But honestly the list doesn't matter because at the root of all the symptoms is the same root: pride.

Israel took God's place on a physical throne. We take God's place on the throne of our hearts. When we unseat the sovereign Lord, we always take His place. And friend, "self" is a terrible king. We trade supreme wisdom for limited knowledge. We trade benevolent rule for selfish ambition. We trade unrivaled authority for temporary control.

> **When we unseat the sovereign Lord, we always take His place.**

In the same way God warned Israel, He is warning us. When we dethrone God, we set ourselves on a path to hard times. It might not look like it now, but the spiral is coming and, like 1 and 2 Kings, it will be hard to get through. If we could see our end play out in a book the way we can with the kings of Israel, we would have a difficult time reading it. I want to learn Israel's lesson. I know my heart, and I know just how selfish I can be. I can't be trusted with a throne. But He can.

A War and a Disease Within

Settling who occupies the throne of our heart matters if we want to be whole, peace-filled, and satisfied. Otherwise we will suffer the chaos of our own internal civil war.

Understanding sanctification reorients everything; yet few of us have ever really studied this super important theological reality. It may sound like a stuffy church word, but I assure you it's more beautiful, relevant, and Christ-exalting than we give it credit for. The goal of this book isn't just to help us understand what sanctification is, but maybe as importantly, *what it is not.* In the day-to-day stuff of life, sometimes it's more helpful to anticipate the traps that get us off track.

Because as we said, one of the differences between self-help and sanctification is in what it produces. I don't know about you, but sometimes it's hard to know what fruit looks like. But frustration? I can see that coming a mile away. It creeps in when I'm tired or hungry. The "hungry" part I can usually address. (Not always wisely, but queso and guac typically do the trick.) You know what I can't seem to fix? How tired I am. Exhaustion breeds frustration. And you know what causes exhaustion? Self-help. Self-help revolves around, rises and falls, and depends on me. How can it not be exhausting?

We discovered in the last chapter that a self-help strategy to spiritual growth has lots of unintended, problematic symptoms. Worse than a placebo, what we think will make us better actually makes us worse. We will look at each of those later. But first, let's deal with the disease.

Embedded deep in our spiritual DNA is an autoimmune disease of sorts. I know a thing or two about chronic illness. I have Crohn's disease. It's not something I caught; it's a genetic mutation that causes my body to see part of my intestines as a foreign invader. My body attacks my gut like a virus, causing pain and inflammation. Untreated, the long-term effects can be catastrophic. In short, my body is fighting against itself, sabotaging my health and wellness.

In a way, we experience the same thing spiritually. When we are made new in Christ, we get a new nature. But our fallenness is still there, and man is it jacked up. Damaged in the garden, none of us are born whole or blameless. Given time, we will give evidence to the brokenness of our spiritual genetic code. And when we receive Christ, that old DNA—our flesh, as the Bible calls it—sees that new nature as foreign. And it fights with all its might against us.

I think this is what Paul is getting at in Romans 7. He is a man whose nature is at war within him. Read Romans 7:15–25:

> I do not understand what I do. For what I want to do I do not do, but what I hate I do. And if I do what I do not want to do, I agree that the law is good. As it is, it is no longer I myself who do it, but it is sin living in me. For I know that good itself does not dwell in me, that is, in my sinful nature. For I have the desire to do what is good, but I cannot carry it out. For I do not do the good I want to do, but the evil I do not want

to do—this I keep on doing. Now if I do what I do not want to do, it is no longer I who do it, but it is sin living in me that does it.

So I find this law at work: Although I want to do good, evil is right there with me. For in my inner being I delight in God's law; but I see another law at work in me, waging war against the law of my mind and making me a prisoner of the law of sin at work within me. What a wretched man I am! Who will rescue me from this body that is subject to death? Thanks be to God, who delivers me through Jesus Christ our Lord!

Look at what Paul is saying. There is an almost automatic response in him, something that resists even the good things that Paul wants to do. He admits that the goodness that lives in him is foreign. It came from Christ upon his conversion. Both of these natures reside in Paul, and those two sides—or as he says in other passages, our "old and new selves"—are fighting against one another. At any given moment, the sin-nature and Christ's nature inside Paul battle for the throne of his heart.

We are at war, Paul says. What causes war? Think back—for some of us way back—to everything you learned about the American Revolutionary War, the Civil War, World War I, World War II, or the Vietnam War. What's the one enduring quality that always precedes

> If there is someone on the throne, we will fight like crazy for that someone to be us.

war? Competing powers that want control. The same is true for us.

Buried there in our sin-nature is a prideful compulsion for control. And that need for control rivals our desire to give God control. We are a people who resist submission. (If you are a wife, you likely know it's true.) If there is someone on the throne, we will fight like crazy for that someone to be us.

You know what is so interesting to me about what Paul is saying? This war happens not in unbelievers but *believers*. We are in the midst of a battle; we are not a peace-time people. But what then of equally true passages like Philippians 4:6–7? (Also written by the apostle Paul, by the way.)

> Do not be anxious about anything, but in every situation, by prayer and petition, with thanksgiving, present your requests to God. And the peace of God, which transcends all understanding, will guard your hearts and your minds in Christ Jesus.

I've quoted and been quoted this passage almost as many times as Jeremiah 29:11. And most often I've flipped for this passage in the midst of drama, hardship, or hurt. I need a Philippians 4:6–7 prescription when life feels less than peaceful. I think that's what Paul intended. Notice what he says about that precious "peace of God." It passes or transcends all understanding. It doesn't make sense. It defies logic. Why? Because God's peace is meant to hold or keep us when life *isn't peaceful*. If God's peace was only present when life was peaceful, it wouldn't pass all understanding. And it likely wouldn't be attributed to the

Lord. His promise of peace is in spite of our circumstances, all those less than peaceful ones.

The peace of God doesn't promise to change our circumstances. It's meant to redefine them. Are you stuck in a catastrophic fallout with your in-laws? God's peace probably doesn't change that, but it can keep your heart from borrowing anxiety about what tomorrow or the next holiday might bring.

Do the unknowns about your future, post-college plans have a choke hold on your todays? The peace of God doesn't immediately land you the perfect job or send that acceptance letter for grad school. But His peace does offer our minds rest from the fear that maybe the future we hoped for isn't going to happen.

Maybe you're struggling with infertility, singleness, unemployment, adultery, addiction, or abandonment. Situations like these don't usually get better with a single prayer. But asking for God's peace can change our perspective on the hard places in which we find ourselves.

Then the hard question is, will we submit our hearts, worries, and emotions to the peace that God promises? Or will we submit our hearts to our own exit strategies, deflective tactics, or schemes to get our way? And again, we are back to the discussion of the war within.

Do you feel at war? Maybe. Maybe not. The shift of putting ourselves on the throne isn't this cosmic, Avengers-style civil war. It's dangerously more subtle.

For good, Bible-believing, holiness-chasing people like us, the temptation isn't to abandon what we believe and turn our backs on God. The temptation is to pursue loving God and looking like Christ *in our own strength*. The temptation is to do all those right things for all the wrong reasons. The danger is to love Jesus but somehow simultaneously make it all about us—to make holiness look a lot like happiness. This disease will attack our family life, cause inflammation in our relationships, hijack our emotional health, and make us too exhausted to be effective for the kingdom.

As you read and think about the idea that we are internally at war, how does that make you feel? Maybe you know, deep in your soul, it's true. Some of us have the war wounds and battle scars to prove it. But perhaps like me, you think that this idea of "war" doesn't just feel wrong; maybe you wonder if it *is* wrong, even unbiblical. After all, aren't there passages about peace and comfort? Haven't we been freed from sin? Are we not free in Christ? Hasn't He "won the war" over sin and death?

> **The danger is to love Jesus but somehow simultaneously make it all about us—to make holiness look a lot like happiness.**

The answer is both yes and no, because it depends on what we mean by *free*.

Friends, sometimes we cherry-pick the Scripture bits about peace, ease, and light burdens and jerk them right out of context, forgetting that many of these passages are actually, *actually*, about how to live well in the midst of stress, strife, and yoke-wearing. Yes, we are free *in* Christ but not *from Christ*. We are not *independent*.

Take one of the more popular passages we flip open to affirm the peaceful, easy life of Christ: "Come to me, all you who are weary and burdened, and I will give you rest. Take my yoke upon you and learn from me, for I am gentle and humble in heart, and you will find rest for your souls. For my yoke is easy and my burden is light."

This is Matthew 11:28–30. Now, I don't know about you, but I'm not super familiar with a yoke. So, I did a little research. A yoke is a curved piece of wood that was fitted to oxen to keep them pulling a plow, cart, or otherwise heavy load. It was affixed using metal rods or a noose of rope around the animals' necks. It was used to keep them from taking an easier path, ignoring the lead of the one driving the plow. Yokes were meant to keep them in line. The more they resisted or struggled, the heavier the yoke felt.

Traditionally, when Scripture refers to a "yoke," it's a symbol of hardship, submission, or servitude. Jeremiah wore a yoke to symbolize his message that Judah should submit to Babylon (Jer. 27–28). Yokes may refer to other burdens or responsibilities, such as sin (Lam. 1:14), service to God (Lam. 3:27; Jer. 2:20; 5:5), or obedience to Torah (Acts 15:10) or Christ (Matt. 11:29–30).

You've probably read it or heard Matthew 11:30 quoted when life gets wicked hard. We love to chant the life-affirming truth that Jesus' yoke is easy and His burden light. But friend, it's still a yoke. His yoke is definitely easier to carry than the world's, but it's still a yoke. In fact, just before saying that His yoke is easy, Jesus has some really strong words for the cities, people, and places that refused to repent and turn to Him. So when Jesus asked us to take His yoke on us, He's inviting us to give up control and surrender to Him. He wants us to learn from Him. To trust His "gentle spirit and humble heart."

He wants us to give up the burden of control and take up the burden of surrender. He doesn't liberate us from a yoke; Jesus exchanges the yoke of the law and religion—things we definitely can't do—for the yoke of His lordship and a relationship with Him—things we were made to do. We are not free to be in control of our lives; we are free to live under His control, trusting His plans and purposes for our lives.

And this is the actual context of Matthew 11, and in fact much of Matthew's Gospel. Matthew writes his Gospel to convince the Jews that Jesus is the King and Messiah they want, but not the one they expected. Jesus came to establish His kingdom, but it would look drastically different than what the Jews had expected. They wanted a military state with Jews finally in control and in possession of their Promised Land. They wanted a political turnover where they were finally in power. Instead, Jesus comes to establish His own kingdom without the use of political force and promise a heavenly home that far exceeds anything they could have ever imagined.

Jesus is explaining that the yoke that the Pharisees and religious leaders have placed on God's people is both hard and heavy.

It is important that we make a distinction here between the law of God and the law that the Pharisees tried to enforce. God gave His people laws in the Pentateuch, the first five books of the Bible—Genesis, Exodus, Leviticus, Numbers, and Deuteronomy. These five books give us the basic laws of God that govern holy living for His people Israel. These laws generally fall into three categories: civil, ceremonial, and moral law.

The civil law governed how the people would behave toward one another in everyday society, sort of like state laws. The ceremonial law defined how an unholy people approach a holy God in worship. The moral law explained how God's people ought to live and act to reflect the character of their holy God. The sum total of these laws numbered 613 and is often called the Mosaic Law. Those laws are actually *Scripture*. But the Pharisees, the religious elite, had added their man-made rules on top of Scripture, trying to forecast every conceivable situation. In our time, it would be like adding the law "never use a credit card" to the Scripture principle to steward your money well. Yes, Scripture calls us to stewardship. But putting our own personal convictions on the level of Scripture itself isn't a good thing. By the time of Christ's ministry, the "law" was full to the brim of examples like this, going far beyond actual Scripture, swelling to an unmanageable, incalculable number. The new laws exchanged God's authority for man's authority and personal preference or conviction for divine law. It was simply too much for the people to bear.[2]

Jesus is saying that He wants to free His people from the burdensome yoke of the Pharisees. Jesus will do this by way of Calvary and His death and resurrection. Jesus satisfies the civil and ceremonial laws. No more blood sacrifices necessary! Nothing separating us from the Most Holy Place where the presence of God resides. He became the perfect spotless lamb, His blood once and for all covering the sins of His people and forever providing a way for us to enter into the Most Holy Place of God. Because of Jesus, we are welcomed in. The burden of the civil and ceremonial laws is no longer required of us, one, because we have our own civil laws in a governmental system far outside the nation of Israel, and, two, because we no longer need ceremonies to enter God's presence. We have Christ for that.

Jesus, though He certainly fulfilled all the moral laws, does not free *us* from the moral law. We are still called to live within the spirit of the law governing how holy people act and reflect a holy God. In that way we are not totally free. Jesus doesn't remove our yoke. He exchanges the heavy, self-promoting, often unfair yoke of the Pharisees for the perfect, loving, tender yoke of Jesus. He holds the reins. He is in control. We are free from the legalities of the law, but we are now governed by His lordship.

Paul talks about this idea in Galatians 3:23–25. "Before the coming of this faith, we were held in custody under the law, locked up until the faith that was to come would be revealed. So the law was our guardian until Christ came that we might be justified by faith. Now that this faith has come, we are no longer under a guardian."

When Paul is writing this to the church in Galatia, I wonder if he was remembering a time that he and his friend Silas had been held in custody under the watch of a real-life guardian. We read the story in Acts 16. Paul and Silas have been imprisoned because of their faithful preaching of the good news about Jesus. They are shackled in the inner cell of the jail and guarded by a jailer. Sometime in the night, a violent earthquake shakes the foundation of the jail and breaks the chains that bound Paul and Silas. When the jailer awakens to find the doors opened and the chains loose, he draws his sword to take his own life. In Roman culture if a prisoner escaped from jail, the jailer was killed as punishment for his negligence. This particular jailer wanted to do the job himself instead of facing the shame that was coming for him.

Paul interrupts the jailer's suicide attempt shouting, "Don't harm yourself. We are all here!" (Acts 16:28). Paul and Silas had been bound to the jail and their jailer. They had no way to release themselves. They had no choice but to stay shackled. Yet, God supernaturally intervenes and frees them. They are bound no more. But rather than flee for freedom, Paul and Silas willingly remain in the jail cell. Why? The Bible doesn't tell us their motives, but it does record the outcome of their sacrifice.

When the jailer realizes that these former prisoners chose to remain restrained, he asks, "Sirs, what must I do to be saved?" (Acts 16:30). Because they chose to stay, the jailer is saved. Paul and Silas had been freed from their bondage, and yet they willingly stayed restrained for the sake of the gospel and the salvation of their jailer. God's glory and will meant more than their freedom.

This is a picture of what Paul is describing in Galatians 3:15–29. Before our faith in Christ, you and I are bound to the law. We had no hope to free ourselves from the duty and obligation of the law. We were called to honor God by faithfully observing every single one of the more than 600 commands of the Mosaic Law. The law kept us shackled to a system that reminded us at every failure that we would never be able to fully obey God and rightly reflect His holy character. The law was and is perfect. We were and are imperfect law keepers.

Like Paul and Silas, we could not free ourselves. But the law births hope, and hope grows faith that one day Someone might come who could fully obey all of God's law. Someone would release us from our slavery to this sacrificial system.

Someone did come, and His name is Jesus.

The law is no longer our guardian, but it is still our guardrail. We are not bound by it anymore, but ignoring God's laws makes us vulnerable. When we willingly crash through the restraints of God's protection, we put our lives in peril. When we submit to God's law, we show that we are a people set apart for the sake of God's glory.

Jesus fully satisfied the law of God, but the regulations that govern morality and personal holiness still reflect God's perfect will for you and me. For the believer, we gladly submit to His ways. Like Paul and Silas, we sacrifice our liberty for the sake of the gospel. Submitting to God's law proves that we trust His tender, loving care more than our freedom or comfort. And, all things considered, we end up seeing that living outside of God's law is actually not freedom at all, but slavery to some other yoke!

> The law is no longer our guardian, but it is still our guardrail.

With that context, let's read that Matthew 11 passage one more time: "Come to me, all you who are weary and burdened, and I will give you rest. Take my yoke upon you and learn from me, for I am gentle and humble in heart, and you will find rest for your souls. For my yoke is easy and my burden is light."

Are you weary from trying to apply God's Word as best you see fit? Are you worn out trying to do what looks holy and impresses people? Jesus is asking us to surrender, learn from Him, humble our hearts to His care, and He in turn promises to give us rest for our souls. It's a sweet invitation to depend on Him, not be independent from Him.

Let's be clear. Jesus places a yoke on us. It's neither abusive nor burdensome. But we still wear a yoke. We are oxen under the yoke of a caring, tender plowman. Or, as Jesus says in other passages, the sheep of His pasture. But make no mistake, at no point are we the plowman or the shepherd.

Set Apart

W hy rabbit-trail about peace and light yokes? What does that have to do with sanctification? Well, nothing actually. And that right there is the problem.

Look back to the questions we answered in chapter 2. What is the endgame of Christianity? My first honest answer was to impress people. But a close second is so that I can have an easy, peace-filled life. Highly Instagram-worthy, and free from drama or stress.

I want to be happy. I bet you do too. But Jesus? Jesus wants us to be holy. Now that's not to say that He isn't concerned with our happiness. He is, but the kind of happiness He's after doesn't hinge on social media followers, how shiplapped our house is, or how many of our bucket list spots we can check off. Jesus wants our marriages to thrive, our careers to flourish, and our kids to be successful, but it's likely that His definition of success in our marriages, careers, and parenting is different than ours.

Remember the list we made highlighting the difference between self-help and sanctification? Self-help pursues happiness above all else. Sanctification is a process and pursuit with pit stops in cross-bearing and sacrifice. Holiness is the endgame. That's why it's helpful to debunk the idea that the Christ-filled life is filled with worldly peace and ease.

Unfortunately, if we pursue pleasure and avoid pain, we will miss most of the processes the Holy Spirit intends to use to make us act, think, and live more like Jesus. Maybe that's not true for you. But man, friend, it's true for me. I spend most of my life avoiding the very things God has historically used to make His people useful and beautiful to Him.

This has always been His pattern. When we study Scripture, all of it—the Old and New Testaments—we see major themes and patterns developing. It began when God called an unknown man named Abram and made him and his descendants into an unknown nation named Israel.

> God calls His people
> to be separate.
> Separate is hard.
> Hard is good.
> God is best.

Every summer our church hosts "Kingdom Camp" for the kids in our little Georgia community. We've been working our students systematically through the Old Testament looking at the Patriarchs, Moses, David, and Daniel. We discovered early on that these stories follow the same key principles. (The Patriarchs are the fathers of the faith: Abraham, Isaac, Jacob, and Joseph.)

Consider these four repeating patterns:

God calls His people to be separate.

Separate is hard.

Hard is good.

God is best.

Let's look at Abram. You probably know him as Abraham because God eventually changed Abram's name. God called Abraham away from Harran (his home country), his family, and everything he'd ever known. And when God called Abraham, He didn't even tell Abraham exactly where He was sending him. Abraham got the simple and not-so-specific instruction that he was to go to "the land I will show you" (Gen. 12:1).

God wanted Abram to be called out from the comfort of his home and family because God had a plan, a master plan, for establishing a people that would be the Lord's. Abram was the beginning of the nation of Israel—a nation of people chosen by God to be in relationship with Him and reflect His character to the world around them. Abram, and later Israel, was called out, or set apart from those around them, uniquely defined and identified as the people of God.

In other words, God wanted them to be *holy.* In the Old Testament, the Hebrew word most often used for "holiness" is *qadosh,* and it means to be set apart or separate. From the beginning, God wanted His people set apart or dedicated to Him. Sin suckered us and broke the separateness God had created us for. The story of Scripture and redemption is how God would buy us back from sin and forever sets us apart for an eternal relationship with Him. His endgame is our holiness, or separate-ness.

If you look at most of the stories of the heroes of the faith— Isaac, Jacob, Joseph, Moses, Joshua, David, Daniel, Esther, Isaiah, Jeremiah, John the Baptist, Peter, and Paul—you can see the same call to be separate. The stories of Scripture are more exciting, harrowing, and thrilling than most Hollywood blockbusters. But this calling out is never easy. To be set apart is to sacrifice what we want. We are called to give up what we have known and cherished. We are invited to crucify our selfish plans and dreams for the better pursuit of what God has planned for us.

Quit Hustling and Let Him Lead

Sanctification isn't purely passive, but it doesn't entirely rest on us either. We learn the sweet dance of letting God lead, while not stepping on His toes or taking over completely. In nearly every story line of Scripture we see men and women learning this dance. God extends an invitation, and they respond.

> We are invited to crucify our selfish plans and dreams for the better pursuit of what God has planned for us.

Reimagine with me the greatest stories of our faith if the heroes of Hebrews 11 had defined holiness the way many of us do. What if Moses had pursued happiness rather than holiness? He would have stayed in the posh, palace life of Egyptian royalty rather than choosing to free God's people. What if Esther had looked to protect her life rather than preserve her people? How differently might the conquest of the Promised Land have been if Joshua had not been strong and filled with courage? Can you imagine David looking at Goliath and choosing to return to the safety of his father's land as a humble shepherd?

But all of these stories begin with God. He is the great Initiator. They didn't dream up their own assignments. Their life's work didn't involve hustle or ambition. Now, let me clarify. Walking with God is often a lot of work. That's what we established earlier. We are still surrendered to the work Christ calls us to. It isn't wrong to desire excellence in service to our King. That's not what we are talking about here. In today's culture, hustle and ambition are usually a subcategory of self-help meant to elevate our position and grab for what we deserve. It's built around entitlement and self. That is the opposite or crossbearing and yoke-wearing.

For the people like David, Esther, Joshua, or Moses, everything God had called them to required surrendering to Him and giving up what they wanted or thought they deserved. The overwhelming truth of Scripture is clear: Sanctification requires surrender. Holiness isn't the pursuit of happiness. Holiness is the pursuit of Christ.

Holiness more often than not brings hardship and heartache. But it's the only way to live the life that God has promised for us. Does that mean that Moses, Esther, Peter, and Paul weren't happy? I don't think so. I think one day when we get to heaven, they'll say that trusting God and learning to love Him first was the greatest adventure of their lives. Easy? No. Worth it? Yes.

Have you ever watched one of those reality television talent shows and seen a contestant come out to perform who clearly is out of his or her league? Like me, do you ever think, *What on earth made her think singing on that stage was a good idea?* So many people have bought into the lie that we can be anything we want to be. With enough hard work and confidence, we can create any reality we imagine for ourselves.

This kind of self-driven ambition can be the beginning of a life marked by persistent manipulations and countless disappointments. Abner was this kind of man.

When we begin 2 Samuel, we learn that King Saul is dead. Any time there is the death of a king, there is usually a scramble for power and position. Second Samuel 3 begins to reveal the selfish ambition that will be Abner's downfall. Abner wants to make himself strong, so he sleeps with Saul's concubine. To sleep with the concubine of a dead king was to assert oneself as the new leader. Abner is trying to take matters into his own hands.

Abner wanted to be all that he could be. He certainly didn't lack confidence or vision. His desire was to make his own name great despite knowing that the Lord had appointed David to be the next king of Israel (v. 10). This is a dangerous condition of self-help. We can be very, very good at looking at where we are and reasoning that God put us here to take advantage of the situation. I don't know that this is what Abner is doing, but I do know it's what I do.

So many of us have quoted the phrase, "God helps those who help themselves." In fact, many assume it's actually a verse in the Bible, which it is not. In church-girl circles where we have been trained to do our part, serve the kingdom, and sacrifice for others, women have become really, really good at doing more than our part in the name of Jesus. Because, as we say, "God helps those who help themselves."

But as we will see with the story of Abner, God usually *doesn't* help those who help themselves. Call it what you want, but that kind of selfish ambition, hustle, or control usually gets folks into trouble. (Believe me, I know.) The truth is that God helps those who *cannot* help themselves! He leans in to help those who have stepped into a God-assignment bigger than they can handle. God helps those who have surrendered their ability to control or manipulate a situation. That's the place where God steps in.

This is not that kind of story, however.

Ish-Bosheth, Saul's son, confronts Abner for this offense. While Abner doesn't deny sleeping with the concubine, his lack of denial is confirmation of his sin. Abner simply asserts his loyalty to David. This is the danger of selfish ambition and self-determination. Driven by desire and confidence, Abner tries to hide his real motives and refuses to admit the truth when he is caught.

Evidence that Abner's manipulation is working, Ish-Bosheth fears Abner and drops the matter. Emboldened by his newfound authority, Abner now goes to David with a plot to try and worm his way into David's inner circle. While David treats him warmly and graciously, David is not naïve. He has not been duped. Second Samuel will chronicle David's extreme loyalty to all of Saul's household.

Abner's actions toward David don't accomplish what Abner so desperately desired.

It would be easy to read this passage and think Abner is just transitioning his loyalty from Saul to David. Any one of these circumstances alone may not indict Abner. But collectively, this passage paints a picture of Abner as a man plagued by selfish ambition that would ultimately be his downfall. Yes, "Abner had been strengthening his own position in the house of Saul" (2 Sam. 3:6).

There is much for us to learn from Abner about ambition and hustle. Abner and David give us two competing pictures of how selfish ambition is never enough to change God's predetermined purpose for each person.

Selfish ambition falls under the umbrella of self-help. It promises what we cannot deliver but depends on us to do it anyway. Sanctification promises what we cannot deliver but trusts God to do it in spite of us. Self-help manipulates others to strengthen our position. Sanctification allows us not to worry about what others' motivations or manipulations are. Like David, we can be gracious because God will do what is right. David was able to be gracious with Abner because he knew the Lord was in control of David's future. Finally, selfish ambition looks out for self while godly ambition is focused on the glory of God.

Ambition in and of itself isn't wrong. We ought to want to be all that God created us to be and to do all that God created us to do. Godly ambition rests in God's sovereignty. But our motives will tell us if we are manipulating a plan or trusting God's purpose. All the hustle in the world can't get us farther than the hand of God can take us or has appointed for us to go.

Like Abner, I've been guilty of hustling to try and make something happen, or to position myself for God's blessing. *If I do this, God will do that*, I've thought. There's a tension there for sure. Sanctification is the process of making us holy, set apart for God. It is the only cure for being sick of me. Only God can do what is needed to make us whole and healthy. He prescribes the medicine, but we have to take it.

> Sanctification promises what we cannot deliver but trusts God to do it in spite of us.

Regeneration, Justification, and Sanctification

Part of the beauty of sanctification is that it's a unique way we work *with* God in the pursuit of Christlikeness. Sanctification is different from equally important theological terms, like regeneration and justification, because sanctification invites us to participate. (This is especially helpful for those of us who want to "do" something, those of us sitting on our hands wanting a fix. This is for all the hustlers.)

Regeneration happens when the Holy Spirit makes us a new creation, resurrecting us from being dead in sin and making us alive in Christ. This process is completely the work of the Holy Spirit, and not dependent on our works at all. John 1:12–13 says, "Yet to all who did receive him, to those who believed in his name, he gave the right to become children of God—children born not of natural descent, nor of human decision or a husband's will, but born of God." This is regeneration. Think of it this way. You and I didn't have any responsibility in our own physical births. The same is true for our spiritual births. You and I cannot manufacture or manipulate regeneration. We respond in faith to the wooing of the Spirit. We bring nothing to the table in regeneration, not our works, not our résumé, not any good thing we have ever done or could do.

This is all and only the grace of God and the goodness of the Holy Spirit. Regeneration is a sweet, sweet word, and a term that's worth understanding. Not so we can use smart words or hang with our seminarian friends. Regeneration reminds us of the goodness of God and our desperate, desperate need for Him to awaken our souls from death. Think Ezekiel and all those dry bones. Life, from death.

But if we lean into regeneration *too* much, we become the people of the "let go and let God" camp. Regeneration, being made alive, is only part of our spiritual identity. Living people live. It is not biblical for us to sit on our hands expecting God to do all the work. In his letter to the Philippians, Paul says it this way: "Continue to work out your salvation with fear and trembling, for it is God who works in you to will and to act in order to fulfill his good purpose" (Phil. 2:12–13). We work out what He works in us. We live out how He's made us alive. Enter sanctification.

Understanding regeneration and sanctification is hard work. But there's still more work to be done. There is a third category that is necessary for our life in Christ. Justification is a term that explains our right, legal standing before God. After the Holy Spirit has made us new in Christ and we have responded in faith, we are legally forgiven before God. The legal transaction where Christ pays for our debts and God the Father declares us free and righteous is the essence of justification. One critical element of evangelical Christianity is the belief that we are justified not by our works or résumé. We can't earn justification; we don't progressively earn a right standing with God by stacking up credits against our debts. We are justified by faith in Jesus and His completed work on the cross.

In his commentary on Romans, Robert H. Mounce says that "faith is the total surrender to the ability and willingness of God to carry out his promises."[3] Consider how Romans 4:20–22 describes Abraham's faith. "Yet he did not waver through unbelief regarding the promise of God, but was strengthened in his faith and gave glory to God, being fully persuaded that God had power to do what he had promised. This is why 'it was credited to him as righteousness.'"

Abraham, the "he" the verse above is describing, certainly lived out this principle. God's promise to Abraham was the substance of his faith.

Most Jews at the time of Paul's letter to the Romans would have passionately argued that Abraham was justified by his works—offering Isaac as a sacrifice or by Abraham's circumcision. Circumcision was an outward expression of Israel's commitment to be set apart from the pagans around them. Jews would point to Abraham, the patriarch of their faith, as a picture of how works earn a right standing before God.

In these first few chapters of Romans, Paul is trying to reframe a commonly held opinion regarding Abraham's faith. Paul's primary argument here is that Abraham was justified by his *faith*, not his works.

So what is justification again? It is a legal declaration that our sins have been paid for by another, and therefore we are not in danger of bearing the punishment our sins deserve. When we are justified we are made right with God. It is God-given faith that activates that deposit or transaction. When Abraham was credited with righteousness by God, he was justified—considered in right standing—before God.

The promise of Abraham being credited righteousness comes from Genesis 15:6, where God restates His promise to make then-Abram into a mighty nation with offspring as numerous as the stars. Ancient Abram and barren Sarai would parent a mighty nation. This promise was made to Abram who was in his eighties married to Sarai (later Sarah) who was well past childbearing age. Yet in that instance, God, who knows men's hearts, saw Abram's faith in that promise and legally made Abram righteous by his faith.

More than a decade before his son Isaac was born and twenty-nine years before his circumcision, Abraham was declared righteous. Abraham's faith and subsequent justification wasn't based on his own works or even on God fulfilling that specific promise. God had yet to make good on His Word and give Abram land or a son. Abraham looked forward in faith and stood firm on the promises of God because Abraham trusted God's character.

It was Abraham's faith in the promise of God, Abraham's faith that God is trustworthy, Abraham's faith that God will not fail that made him righteous before God.

Where Abraham looked forward in faith, we have the unbelievable blessing of looking back in faith at the finished work of Jesus Christ! What God promised, He fulfilled! And we can live in the sweet assurance that what Jesus did on the cross was sufficient to make us legally innocent before God.

Romans 3:25–28 says it this way,

> God presented Christ as a sacrifice of atonement, through the shedding of his blood—to be received by faith. He did this to demonstrate his righteousness, because in his forbearance he had left the sins committed beforehand unpunished—he did it to demonstrate his righteousness at the present time, so as to be just and the one who justifies those who have faith in Jesus. Where, then, is boasting? It is excluded. Because of what law? The law that requires

> works? No, because of the law that requires
> faith. For we maintain that a person is justified
> by faith apart from the works of the law.

Justification makes us legally right before God, now and forever because it rests not on us but on Jesus. We cannot undo what He has done; therefore, we can't undo what His death, burial, and resurrection secure for us. But if we lean too hard into justification without the balance of sanctification, we become people unconcerned with holy living, only holy dying. "Heaven is secure for us, so live in grace and freedom." This is the "free in Christ" camp. I'd argue it's the cultural Christianity camp that talks about Jesus, love, and acceptance. The camp that doesn't need to wrestle down the real implications of holiness and what it means to be set apart.

Our justification doesn't just secure us heaven; it brings heaven here. Justification ought to ignite something in us. The justified of God are a people living in a holy "now and not yet." Heaven is our home, not this place, but we live out the kingdom principles of grace and gospel here so that others

Holy people live holy lives.

can see Jesus on display in us. Holy people live holy lives.

Peter charges us as holy people to live like the priests of the Old Testament who represented and reflected God.

> But you are a chosen people, a royal priesthood,
> a holy nation, God's special possession, that you
> may declare the praises of him who called you
> out of darkness into his wonderful light. Once

you were not a people, but now you are the people of God; once you had not received mercy, but now you have received mercy. Dear friends, I urge you, as foreigners and exiles, to abstain from sinful desires, which wage war against your soul. Live such good lives among the pagans that, though they accuse you of doing wrong, they may see your good deeds and glorify God on the day he visits us. (1 Pet. 2:9–12)

Regeneration or justification without understanding your part in sanctification can lead to a lukewarm lifestyle or laziness. On the flip side, sanctification without a right understanding of regeneration and justification leads to legalism.

Regeneration and justification rest on the goodness and grace of God and the finished work of Jesus. But sanctification? Sanctification begins during regeneration but is not completed in this life. God sanctifies us through the Holy Spirit, His Word, discipline, His church's involvement in our lives, and our circumstances, to name a few. However, we respond in obedience and active cooperation pursuing God's will, God's way. Regeneration and justification make us holy. Sanctification lets us *live* holy.

> Regeneration and justification make us holy. Sanctification lets us *live* holy.

This three-leg stool of regeneration, justification, and sanctification provides the stable base upon which our faith rests. Lean too much on any one, and the seat becomes unstable. I can tell you I've toppled over and ended up on my rear more than a few times.

The sickness of "me"—that self-centeredness that saps my spiritual energy and keeps me trying but not growing—is the result of this imbalance. Sometimes I'm far too complacent, resting on a work that isn't mine but not letting it produce the fruits of love, joy, peace, patience, kindness, goodness, faithfulness, self-control. I don't walk in good works; I rest too much on "grace." Other times, I forget that I am already holy and right before God. I forget that that holiness has a purpose and outworking. I do this all the while hustling—not out of love or devotion, but out of duty and desperation to keep up appearances.

Holiness doesn't just set us apart *from* something, but also sets us apart *to* Someone. As we said, we aren't free in the way the world defines freedom. We don't sign a declaration of *in*dependence, but rather a declaration of *de*pendence. God's holiness has with it the expectation that we honor Him in a way that rightly reflects His character. Christ's holiness is transferred to us, but we are to be transformed by it.

Filling the Void

When we are set apart, we have to fill the space with affection and devotion to God. Because being separate always leaves a hole. If we don't fill that hole with the Lord, we will fill it with an idol. None of us leave that space empty. It's what we talked about earlier. We will fill the throne. And can I be honest? More often than not, I fill that void with my own vain attempts to control my life.

Are you a January 1st resolution maker? I used to be. And then I got so sick of making the same resolutions year after year. Self-discipline is not my strong suit. Actually, the issue isn't that I'm not disciplined. It's that I'm not good at self-denial. I can make myself do lots of things. Stopping myself from doing things, that's the problem.

I don't like to do without. If there is empty time, I fill it. If there is a pit in my stomach, I'll fill it. If there is a hole in my soul, I'll find an idol. If I'm insecure, I'll look for ways to compensate. This is a dangerous, dangerous vice.

In Leviticus 10:1–2, we get a sober picture of two men who filled in a place reserved for the Lord. "Aaron's sons Nadab and Abihu took their censers, put fire in them and added incense; and they offered unauthorized fire before the LORD, contrary to his command. So fire came out from the presence of the LORD and consumed them, and they died before the LORD."

Just two chapters earlier, Leviticus 8 ends with this affirming verse, "So Aaron and his sons did everything the LORD commanded through Moses" (Lev. 8:36). What an unbelievable compliment. Only a few people in Scripture get this kind of credit. Yet only a short time later, the fire of God's judgment kills those same sons of Aaron for failing to follow God's rules and honoring His holiness.

Leviticus 10 says Nadab and Abihu put fire in their censers. Some scholars suggest that the sons may have used common fire as opposed to the holy fire sent by God. This would certainly reveal they lacked a proper reverence for God's unique and holy flame.

Perhaps the offense was that they offered the wrong recipe of incense. In Exodus 30:9 God warned Aaron of using common incense of the altar, "Do not offer on this altar any other incense or any burnt offering or grain offering, and do not pour a drink offering on it."

Based on certain commentaries on Leviticus 16:1–2, it's also possible that the sons went into the Most Holy Place. This area in the interior of the tabernacle was reserved only for the high priest and only on the Day of Atonement. They violated God's restrictions and permissions for entering His presence.

While the exact details of the offense are unclear, God's judgment is certain. He kills Nadab and Abihu. Their unauthorized fire—however they went about it—elicits His authorized fire.

What happened between Leviticus 8 and Leviticus 10? The sons were commended along with Aaron and then just a bit later struck down by God's fair and perfect justice? How could they slip so far in just a few short hours? I don't know for sure, but I think we can infer some conclusions about their hearts and ours.

Perhaps they wrongly believed that after being set apart for God's work in the priesthood, they could live like they wanted. *Well, whew, we made it to God's good side. Now that He's given us His favor and made us the leaders, I suppose we can take a breather and go about things the way we deem best.* Sound familiar? Many of us believe that we are free from the law, promised heaven, and loved by Jesus, we can live any way we want.

But once we become the Lord's, once we are made a part of His "royal priesthood" (1 Pet. 2:9), our lives are not our own. We are bound out of love to serve, honor, and obey Him. We will never be released from this glad obligation. This is a sobering reminder for all of us who seek to draw near to God; He has specific and righteous requirements for how we represent Him to others. The ceremonial duties are certainly different, but the expectation that we ought to be holy because He is holy has not changed (Lev. 11:45). We are set apart to Him and set aside for His work.

We can't just randomly fill the voids created by God's call to be separate. When God's call leaves a hole in our lives, it's likely because He intends for that hole to make us more holy. But if we selfishly stuff it with stuff that's not of Him, we will miss the lessons and growth that separateness intended. Sanctification is the process God uses to make us more like Christ. While sanctification will produce spiritual gifts and spiritual maturity, God first creates the space for those fruits to grow by removing us from people, situations, and habits that keep us from growth. Sanctification often begins with subtraction, not addition.

Separate Is Hard, Hard Is Good, God Is Best

Voids in our lives are often purposeful. God uses our disappointments. He may want us to see that what filled the void originally was less than His ideal for us. Perhaps He wants us to experience that filling that void ourselves will only compound our heartaches. Maybe God wants us to believe that each void can only be fully satisfied by Him. Each lesson is unique for sure, but each lesson has one thing in common. More often than not, the learning of it is just plain hard.

But can I share something that may make thriving through the process a bit easier? God is usually working us through the same steps over and over again. And when you know the process, it's easier to cooperate with Him and not get slowed down resisting what God wants to do. As He sanctifies us, God calls us to be separate. We discover that being separate is hard, that hard is good, and, ultimately, that God is best. We just worked through proof that God calls His people to be separate. Now, let's camp out in the other parts of the process.

Separate Is Hard

One of the greatest surprises about motherhood was how differently each of our four boys act. When Dylan, number two, came along I thought, *I've got this down. I've already raised Cooper, his older brother,* I reminded myself. Sure, two would be harder. Double the work. But at least this time I knew what to expect. Y'all, I was a great mom *before* I had kids. Tell me I'm not alone. Didn't we have it all figured out when we were the sideline spectators? Yes, I knew exactly how I would parent. Oh, how the Lord humbles the proud because, friend, He gave me Dylan. And he could not have been more different than Cooper.

So, when Ryder came along I knew a bit of what to expect. But even then I thought, *Well, I've got two boys now.* I knew he'd be different. But surely, he is going to be some unique combination of the two boys I had already. *I'll see a dash of Dylan mixed in with the cocktail of Cooper and I'll know what to do,* I thought. I grossly underestimated the creative genius of our God (and the infinite permutations of genetic code). Ryder was and is nothing like his older brothers.

Then came Tate.

Y'all, I have four boys. Let that just sink in for a minute. I live in a house with all men. I think God just knew I was simply enough estrogen for any one house, and then He overcompensated just a bit. And before you hit me with the, "Well, you won't have to pay for any weddings" platitude, let me just say that with a thirteen-year-old, I am just beginning to calculate what it will take to feed this tiny army of men until they "leave and cleave." Mercy!!! They are NEVER full. I will have paid for several, lavish, four-course wedding receptions by the time they move out. *Jesus, multiply the loaves and the fish.*

Like each of his brothers before him, Tate is his own little, unique person. Unlike any of the other boys, Tate has always wanted to be with Chad and me. Like right up under us. Right where we are. If we were getting ready in the morning, we always had a tiny audience of one. Ever our shadow, Tate follows us around, talking, asking questions, or just enjoying our presence. It's sweet. Until it isn't. Sometimes I used to think the kid was omnipresent. He was everywhere I went.

Before I had kids, I used to hear moms talk about wanting to go to the bathroom alone. How anytime they tried to "go," their kids would follow. I would think, *Lock the door.* Now I shake my head at my naïve, know-it-all self. Thirteen years of motherhood and I know that when you close the door, they bend down low to talk through the crack and shove their tiny, sweet fingers under it trying to claw their way in. Y'all, it takes all the Jesus in me not to step on those sweet fingers. It's special. It really is.

Truth is, I kind of get it. I get lonely too, and I'm an introvert. You see there's a difference in choosing to be alone and being left out. Being alone is different than being lonely. One you choose. One is chosen for you. I love going to eat by myself or shopping alone. I mean I get giddy when I think about an all-day stay at Panera or my favorite café or Mexican joint. Don't feel bad for me if you see me at one of these places with my earbuds in, reading a book while I snack on chips and queso. I'm not sad about it. Not at all.

But that's a totally different feeling than realizing all your friends went to dinner and you didn't get an invite or sitting alone in church. Or not having a date for New Year's Eve. Or not having girls for a girls' night out. Or finding out a bunch of your friends started a Bible study together and didn't invite you. That kind of lonely is hard. It can bore a hole in your soul that you don't quickly forget.

And if it's happened before, well, that's like re-breaking a healed but weakened bone. That feeling rushes from memory, and you know it the minute it happens.

When I was a freshman in high school, my two best friends had made the cheerleading squad and I had not. Now I wasn't the best cheerleader, so it wasn't a big shock. I was the squishy girl that helped meet the "base" quota for our middle school squad. No biggie. Every girl can't be a top or "flyer" or whatever they call them now. I was okay. Really. It wasn't my life, and I was super happy for Beth and Anna. They were amazing. Like legit. I was just a girl who liked the uniform.

They had spent their summer before our ninth-grade year hanging out with all the junior and varsity cheerleaders. Beth and Anna were the most loyal kinds of friends. Catching me up on all that happened at camp, previewing the newest cheers and dances for me, they did their level best to make sure I didn't feel left out.

But then it happened.

One day at lunch the girls invited me to sit with them. All the cheerleaders were there together at the cheerleader table. (I probably should have known better.) Over the summer each girl had been given a nickname by the older girls. Beth and Anna had given me one as well. When one of the varsity cheerleaders heard Beth call me my wanna-be cheerleader nickname, the older cheerleader spun on her stool and said, "You can't call her that. Those are just for cheerleaders."

I can close my eyes and I remember it all. The smell of cafeteria pizza, French fries, and lunchroom table disinfectant all come rushing back. I can see the look on her face. The look on everyone else's face. What she was wearing. What I was wearing. I promise my cheeks get hot at the thought.

And you guys, the girl that said those words isn't vile or unkind. I know her as an adult. (That's the advantage of small-town life; memories run deep.) She did what a lot of us do as teenagers, speak before we think. Goodness, I do it as an adult. It's not worth being hurt or mad at her about. If she knew, I'm sure she'd feel awful. I'm sure she doesn't remember, and I'm glad. I'd hate to have to replay in my mind all the careless, hurtful things I've stupidly said.

I was sad, ashamed, and aware that things with Beth and Anna probably wouldn't ever be the same. And they weren't. It wasn't their fault. It wasn't even the varsity cheerleader's fault. I just wasn't a part of their group, and there wasn't anything that was going to change that.

I never sat with them again, and I never forgot how it feels to have "alone" chosen for you. I sat by myself at lunch often back then, not by choice but because I wasn't one of them. So yes, I get what it's like to be lonely.

It was a hard season for me. I remember a conversation with my mom back then. Curled up on my white, iron daybed, I was tearfully asking my mom why God had taken away my friends and kept me from making the cheerleading squad. She did what great mothers do, listened, pulled the tear-dampened hair and tucked it behind my ear, and said, "I don't know, sweetie."

"But I will tell you," she said, "that when God does something that seems to hurt, there's always a reason. We may not know why, but I promise, I promise, He loves you. Even more than I do."

I don't mind telling you, it was hard. I was lonely. I didn't get invited to the same parties. I wasn't a part of the cool group.

There were times I didn't care. It would have been hard to try and be cool, when I can tell you categorically, I was not. But there were other times that I wished God had a different plan for me.

But just as Mom said, eventually, I did realize why God had called me out and set me apart. It was for my protection. It's not because I was special. It's because, if I'm really honest, I was weak. For me to learn the lessons I'd need later, separate was the only way. But that, at times, felt unbearably hard. But being separate also made me stronger. Being alone helped me hear the Lord's voice better. Being on the outside helped me see a bigger picture. Most of those lessons weren't easy, but each was necessary and priceless.

I could have ignored the Lord, pushed my way in, and fixed a temporary problem. I could have been happy. But it wouldn't have made me more holy. No. God's calling for me to be separate did that. He was sanctifying me. And it was a lesson that I'd need over and over in the years that followed. And He's sanctifying you too, right there in the middle of your unique circumstances, whether you happen to be at the cool kids table or not. He's using it all to change you.

God calls His people to be separate, and separate is hard. This pattern appears over and over in Scripture. Moses was called out from Egypt, alone in the desert for forty years before returning to emancipate God's chosen people from their slave masters. Joseph was set apart and alone in a pit, a prison, and later a palace while God was preparing him to serve the Pharaoh and save young Israel from famine.

If you were to look at each of the saints listed in Hebrews 11, often called the Hall of Faith, you'd see that each individual was called out of the life he or she had planned in order to pursue God's plan for him or her.

New growth rarely happens in old places. When God plucks us up, sets us apart, and transplants us elsewhere, it forces us out of comfort and into change.

Every year I go and buy flowers from one of those big box stores. I love ferns and annuals on our front porch and back deck. All of my new tenants will live in a pot or container of some kind. I'm not really a green thumb, primarily because I am lazy. I don't even attempt perennials because they won't live up to their namesake. Not under my care.

> New growth rarely happens in old places.

But last year I got ambitious. Rather than just set the pot of flowers in a container, I actually transplanted them into a pot filled with dirt to grow. I carefully cut away the cheap, flimsy, black container they came in and buried the plant in fresh, loose soil. It was messy and hard. And honestly, I wasn't 100 percent sure that I wasn't killing my new plants in the process.

But you know what? They all thrived! My front porch and deck flowers were prettier than they had ever been before. I later discovered that in years past my plants had likely become root-bound. Because I left my ferns in the too-small, less-than-ideal pot they came in, their roots had nowhere to go as they grew. So, they dug in, and tangled themselves around one another. For a fern, a cramped mess of roots underneath can ultimately cause it to strangle itself, stunting its own growth. My fern didn't die. It was still nice to look at, but it wasn't growing or flourishing.

I bet some of us are root-bound. We are still green, but we're not growing. We've dug in and refused the Lord's transplanting of us. Is it just me? We are alive, but we aren't thriving. That's not what God intended for you or for me. I know it. And I bet you do too. This is why I think dealing with the internal process of sanctification is absolutely necessary for growth.

Unfortunately, most of us are more accustomed to checking the leaves or blooms and ignoring the roots. We wrongly assume growth is evidenced by what we can see. In truth, growth happens in the dark, in the dirt, in the hidden places. But by the time you see the flowers, the dirty, productive work has been done. So, when it comes to our spiritual growth, if we don't examine the roots and be open to the discomfort of a transplant, repotting, or cutting away, we won't see progress. And I bet, you'd like a little spiritual progress, right? Man, I would. I don't just want to look good on the outside. I want to actually be growing. And I think, maybe for the first time in my life, I'm willing for Him to do whatever it takes to give me the space (and discomfort) I need to grow. I'm willing for Him to dig me up, set me apart, and transplant me elsewhere if that's what it takes to develop spiritual maturity.

Hard Is Good

When I was in high school I was rarely invited to anything that the cool kids were doing. I knew about the field parties and the concerts and all the things, but I was never a part of that circle. But my senior year, a big group of friends were planning an after-prom party. One guy's parents had decided to host all the kids after we got back from prom. And I was invited to go with my boyfriend. It was the last few weeks of my senior year. I really, really wanted to go. But I knew there would be a fair amount of drinking going on.

If there is a benefit of being on the outside of that cool circle, it's that I'd never been pressured to drink. It wasn't a temptation for me. I wasn't really anxious about being asked, like ever. Most of my friends knew what my personal convictions were.

Again, please know that this was part of the protection of being separate. In those early years of high school, establishing which social group you are part of seems so, so important. And I was on the outside. Temptation is less tempting when you're far removed from it. And because of the Lord's protection of me, I was known as the "good girl." Don't be impressed, being called the good girl was rarely said with respect or admiration. Usually it was kind of a dig, but I got used to it. High schoolers are not typically impressed with the straight-laced goody-goody. But I tell you all this because I don't want you to think I was this super Christian. I wasn't. But I was very, very safely protected. Not by my choice most of the time, but safe nonetheless.

So back to the party. Now I had a decision to make. Having never had the need or the experience, I wasn't a girl who had developed the skill to successfully lie to my parents. I am woefully transparent to them. I told them all about the party and asked their opinion. I told them I wouldn't drink, and I thought I could go and maybe be a Christian witness at the party. (That wasn't likely, but I thought it sounded good.)

Mom and Dad said they trusted me to make a good decision. But Dad then offered some advice. "You can go to the party. And I do trust you to make good, wise decisions about your behavior. But know this. Being a witness for Jesus won't mean just not drinking. I'd expect you to give a reason for why you're not drinking or participating in other activities. When you are with people who don't share your faith, you are either on their agenda or they are on yours. There is rarely an in-between. So, I'd ask you to think about whether or not you can go and be a vocal, intentional witness for Jesus. Mom and I will support whatever you decide."

Ugh. Good advice to hear. Hard advice to live out.

Hard is good, though.

I didn't go to that party. Mostly because I chickened out, and because I didn't think drunk teenagers would be super receptive to this "goody-goody" sharing the gospel. But I know what Dad meant. Even though I was too immature to implement it at the time, the principle stuck with me. Hard things are good things. Hard things push us outside of ourselves and force us to listen and lean on the Holy Spirit whose strength is made perfect in our weakness (2 Cor. 12:5–9).

Maybe you are far braver than me. Maybe you thrive in difficult seasons. But I think that makes you the exception. Most of us run from and resist those tough assignments, invitations, and hard seasons. We generally avoid the very circumstances and situations that God wants to use to make us more like Christ.

And the degrees of hard things that God asks us each to do is as different as each of us. Maybe missing the after-prom party doesn't sound super hard. Or maybe it does. Or perhaps your hard call is refusing to cheat when everybody else is. Maybe God wants you to forgive that friend that hurt you. Perhaps your hard thing is finally saying "yes" to that thing you know God wants you to do. It's possible the difficult thing

God is asking you to do is say "no" to that guy who really, really expects you to say "yes."

In each situation, the call is not an easy one. We may fail the test we didn't cheat on. Our friend may not receive our forgiveness; that friendship may not survive. It's possible that thing you say "yes" to is more than you bargained for. (In my experience it usually is.) And dear, sweet friend who fights for purity, that guy may not stay.

But our hard things aren't meant to make life easier; they are meant to make our faith stronger. Suffering is a significant part of sanctification. And like most of sanctification, suffering includes us but isn't about us.

One of the things I love about Scripture is that it isn't simply a feel-good story, edited with just the highlights and always-winning heroes. No. There's more than a little bit of suffering. No man, save Jesus Christ, has ever suffered like Job. Let me give you a little background if you haven't read Job. Because let's be real. It's not your bedtime story book of the Bible.

Job has lost each of his children, his livelihood, wealth, and eventually his health. And all of this happened with God's permission. As Job grieves, his friends Eliphaz, Bildad, and Zophar all come to mourn with and comfort him. In time they all offer their own opinions of what is happening in Job's life.

It's dangerous to pull Scripture verses out of context and present them as the Truth of God. And the book of Job is a perfect example of this. Just a caveat, always remember that the Bible sometimes records things that God does not approve of. That's the case with most of Job's friends' speeches.

Read Job 4:7–8: "Consider now: Who, being innocent, has ever perished? Where were the upright ever destroyed? As I have observed, those who plow evil and those who sow trouble reap it." This is his friend Eliphaz's argument.

Eliphaz is the first friend to speak, but his argument is similar to Bildad's and Zophar's, which come later. The three friends' speeches all feature four basic assertions. First, they affirm God is sovereign, meaning God is in complete control of everything. Second, they assert God is just and good. Third, they argue that God blesses those who are good and punishes those who are disobedient. Fourth and finally, the "comforters" claim that if one experiences blessings, it's the result of good behavior. Conversely if one experiences hardship or tragedy, something bad has been done to justify that kind of judgment.

On the surface, this might seem logical. However it fails to take into account God's complete character. Eliphaz misses a full understanding of God's goodness and how He demonstrates His goodness toward His people. God's goodness or grace toward us is unmerited, meaning we don't deserve or earn it. He isn't kind toward us because we are worthy; He is kind to us because *He* is worthy.

> If blessing is meant to show us that He is *worthy*, suffering is meant to show us He is *trustworthy*.

This matters because if blessing isn't about us, *then suffering isn't either.* If blessing is meant to show us that He is *worthy*, suffering is meant to show us He is *trustworthy.*

For the people of God, suffering has a higher purpose than how it impacts our lives. Suffering reveals something about God to the world. Job didn't suffer perfectly, but he did suffer well. When we suffer well, it is evidence that God is more valuable and trustworthy than wealth, health, and even family. Perhaps suffering well means that we don't lash out at others even though we are in pain. Maybe suffering well means that we stay in a job where our boss is out to get us, but we persevere in the love and grace of Jesus. Suffering well might look like consistently showing up to worship even when we don't feel well.

The living of suffering isn't nearly as tidy as the teaching of it. I sincerely believe that suffering serves a higher purpose, but suffering is still suffering. And it's messy. The book of Job gives us a glimpse of what it's like when we wrestle through the wreckage of heartache. Suffering is inevitable and hard. But it's not forever or hopeless.

When Chad and I had been married a few years, we bought a house about forty-five minutes from our family and church home because it was closer to our places of work. But in 2008, after driving forty-five minutes to church and small group several times a week, we felt God calling us to move back to our home town closer to our families, friends, and church.

(It's fair to add that we had our first two sons by 2008, I was pregnant with the third, and we had learned the first rule of parenting. Free childcare. Dear younger married couples who swear you'll never move back home, mark my words. Grandparents become super, super valuable. Believe me when I say proximity to backup will trump all those "other" things you love.)

Anyway, we put our house on the market in 2008. Hey homeowners, remember 2008? Remember when you had all that equity in your house or all that cash in your 401K? Yes, we decided to sell in 2008. A few months later the real estate bubble burst, and the United States plummeted into a deep, deep recession.

Two years and multiple deep cuts in price later, I was broken-hearted. You see, we had once again fallen in love with a house only to be told that just hours earlier someone else had put a contract on it. All while our house hadn't moved. It broke me. I remember we were visiting my parents when we found out about our latest contract disappointment. I sat in shock on the carpeted floor in my parents' den. I didn't cry; my tears had dried up. I had moved past sadness into anger.

Have you ever heard someone say, "I don't know how people go through life without believing in God?" I have. And I know what they mean. But I was in a season of life where I kept thinking it would have been easier if I didn't believe in God. I know that's not something polite church girls say. But it's true.

You see, I never doubted that God was in control. I was sure of it. I never, ever wondered if He had the power to change our circumstances. I knew He did. What gutted me was the absolute certainty that God had the power to ease my pain but that *He chose not to.*

Do you know that feeling? I bet you do. And I'm so, so sorry. Many of you have wept because God didn't fix your spouse or marriage. More than a few of you have buried someone you love because God chose not to physically heal. I bet if we were together we could all share a story or two of ways that God didn't act the way we wanted Him to. We'd share solutions that would have been so easy, that would have made so much sense, but that weren't in God's plan. It can be paralyzing.

When we are in those sanctifying situations, the main cry of our heart is "Why, God?"

"Why would You do this to me?"

"What did I do to deserve this?"

"Why aren't You answering my prayers?"

Sound familiar? Maybe you've asked God those same hard questions. When we were in that dark, dark season of 2008–2010, I asked all of those questions. And because of my pain, I spent a lot of time in the book of Job.

Back to the brokenhearted girl who had collapsed on to the carpeted floor of her parents' house. In that moment, I felt hopeless. I didn't know for sure that my faith would survive this season. I didn't think I would stop believing in God. But I was afraid that I wouldn't be able to think about Him the same way. What I was going through was altering how I felt about God and my faith.

I remember that Thursday night like it was yesterday. You see, the next day I was scheduled to get on a plane and go speak to a group of college students in Texas, and I didn't want to go. It wasn't that I didn't want to love on those girls or spend time with them. It was that I was afraid they'd see me for the fraud I felt like I was.

I looked up at my dad and said, "I don't know how I'll get through this weekend. Nothing in me feels all the things I'll be teaching. I know what I'm teaching is true, but I don't feel the truth. My heart isn't in it, and I feel so fake pretending."

Dad said something that night that has profoundly shaped my faith over the last few years. "Sometimes the bravest thing a believer can do is choose to act on what she knows to be true about God, not what she feels about God. And that isn't fake. It's faith."

It isn't fake. It's faith.

"Sometimes the bravest thing a believer can do is choose to act on what she knows to be true about God, not what she feels about God. And that isn't fake. It's faith."

Friend who's faking it, let that truth fall over you. Let it sink down deep. You aren't being fake. You are being faithful. Don't give up. Don't despair. Stay the course. Every time we choose to crack open our Bible when all we want to do is stay in bed and weep over how broken everything feels, it's faith. When we show up and force ourselves to worship even when we are mad at our situation, it's faith. When we pray for that friend that has deeply wounded us, we say to God, "I believe You are who You say You are."

Dad added this, "If you do that long enough, I promise eventually your feelings will catch up with your faith."

So I got on that plane. I told those girls the hard, hard season I was in. I cried. I didn't pretend to be strong. But I did tell the truth. And in the telling of it, I grabbed a hold of it with both hands. I clung to His goodness and unwavering kindness toward His children. I claimed biblical promise after biblical promise, long before they felt like realities in my life. And you know what? Eventually my feelings did catch up. Eventually it didn't feel fake to raise my hand in worship. My faith built my feelings. And I am ever so glad it wasn't the other way around.

Because my faith isn't based on a feeling. My faith is based on an unchanging, immovable God who never wavers or changes. Yes, God calls His people to be separate. Separate is hard. But hard is good, and God is best.

God Is Best

All this would be easier to make peace with if we knew what God was doing and when He intended to turn this hard season around, right? There's this scene in an old episode of *Seinfeld* that involves Kramer trying to help people find a movie they want to see. If you happen to be younger than twenty, we used to have to look up movie times either in the newspaper or by calling an automated message for the theater we wanted to visit. Archaic, right? Well Kramer decides to help prospective movie-goers find their movie time by acting as Moviefone service. (Apparently his number was one digit different than the line for the actual movie theater.) When Kramer's phone rings, he asks people (in his Moviefone voice) to punch in the first few letters of the movie they want to see. Kramer quickly discovers that he can't discern what movie they want from the random "beep" tones that each unique digit produces. It's hilarious to watch. But my favorite line is when after exasperating and unsuccessful attempts, he says, "Why don't you just tell me the movie you want to see?"

I'm not even lying when I tell you that I have in my prayer time said to God, "Why don't You just tell me what You want and what You are doing" in my best Kramer voice. Have you been here? When wrestling with a call or command of God, have you ever wished God would just tell you exactly what was going to happen before you obeyed Him? I've often thought that I could follow God's ways if I knew more details about my future and God's plans. What is He going to do with this suffering? I'd like to think that I could persevere better if I knew what He was doing. But what if that's not necessarily the case? Are we more obedient when we know what's in our future? Maybe not.

Often in Scripture, God doesn't give a ton of details when He asks a person to follow Him in faith. Abraham was told to go to a place that God would show him. Abraham was told to sacrifice Isaac. Esther was to save her people. Peter was supposed to get out of the boat. But in Deuteronomy 28, we see God give clear and carefully defined instructions and consequences that will determine their future. Follow Me, and I will bless you, He promises. Ignore My ways and I will curse you, God declares.

As they move into the Promised Land, God is telling them exactly what their future holds—blessings or curses. More than that, in shocking detail, He describes *how* He will bless or curse Israel in their future, depending on their actions. We could hope that all these details about their future would motivate Israel to be faithful.

If Israel will obey God's commands and listen to His voice, He will:

- bless them in the city and in the field
- bless the fruit of their womb
- bless their cattle, herds, and livestock
- bless them in all of their going and coming
- bless them with plentiful rain and bountiful harvest

- bless them with protection from their enemies
- bless them with prosperity and fame

But if Israel turns away from God's voice, ignoring His commands, then He will:

- curse them in the city and in the field
- curse their wombs, herd, flocks, and fruit
- curse them in their going and coming
- curse them with the afflictions of the Egyptian plagues
- curse them by subjecting them to military defeat, enslavement, and oppression
- curse them with boils, sores, and pestilence

Sadly, though they knew exactly what God was up to, the Israelites made wrong choices. They would not remain faithful, even when their future was all mapped out.

Knowing the details didn't foster obedience. Israel knew exactly what it would cost them and their children (and generations after them) to turn away from God. As you and I wrestle with the choice to obey God, to stick out our hard seasons, let's remember Israel. The unknown can be paralyzing, but knowing the details of what God is up to doesn't necessarily move our faith forward. In the end, obedience is a choice. Obedience isn't based on a certain future; obedience is based on our certain God.

God calls His people to be separate. Separate is hard. Hard is good, and God is best. God doesn't want our confidence to be in the details He supplies. God doesn't want us to be confident just in His promises. Faith isn't the substance of seeing things all mapped out in front of us; it's the substance of things *not* seen. So known details obviously don't foster faith. God wants our confidence built on His character—to believe that banking on future details isn't best, but that banking on *Him* is best. But this kind of confidence is only constructed in those hard moments.

> Obedience isn't based on a certain future; obedience is based on our certain God.

I know it seems cyclical, but if we lose sight of any one of these steps of God's sanctifying process, we will be tempted to find the path of least resistance where quick-fix solutions abound. Places where we can lay down our crosses. Cross-bearing is Christ exalting, and as we will see in the next section, Christ is the ultimate example of satisfaction in God.

Jesus, Our Example of Choosing God as Best

Jesus' entire ministry was aimed at the cross and in anticipation of the resurrection. But those two history-altering realities were not just about you and me. We often describe them with platitudes like "Jesus went to the cross for me." And we will sing songs that talk about the cross's benefit for us. This isn't wrong. But it's only part of the purpose of the cross.

In His final hours before the cross, Jesus prayed in the Garden of Gethsemane. Look at the substance of His prayer from John 17:1–5:

Jesus spoke these things, looked up to heaven, and said: "Father, the hour has come. Glorify your Son so that the Son may glorify you, since you gave him authority over all flesh, so that he may give eternal life to everyone you have given him. This is eternal life: that they may know you, the only true God, and the one you have sent—Jesus Christ. I have glorified you on the earth by completing the work you gave me to do. Now, Father, glorify me in your presence with that glory I had with you before the world existed." (CSB)

Jesus' desire was to bring glory to the Father. God's glory was His best, His highest joy and greatest desire. Did we benefit? Without question. Were we on His mind? Praise His name, yes. But notice what verse 4 says. Saving us was the work, but God's glory was the reason. Jesus wanted God's glory above all else, and it led Him to the cross.

In Scripture David is often referred to as a type of Christ. A "type" is a prophetic symbol of something or someone that will be revealed fully in the future. As a shepherd and king, David is a type of savior for Israel that prefigures Christ. In 1 Samuel 26 we see that David experienced a moment similar to what Jesus faces in Gethsemane. First Samuel 26:8 says, "Abishai said to David, 'Today God has delivered your enemy into your hands. Now let me pin him to the ground with one thrust of the spear; I won't strike him twice.'"

As Jesus prays in the Garden of Gethsemane and prepares for the cross, Judas, a detachment of soldiers, and some officials from the chief priests and Pharisees come to arrest Him. Jesus' loyal friend and disciple, Peter, jumps to defend Jesus and cuts off the ear of one of the soldiers. Jesus says, "Put your sword away! Shall I not drink the cup the Father has given me?" (John 18:11). Jesus would not let Peter's loyalty lead Him outside the will of the Father. And Jesus' assignment was the cross.

In 1 Samuel 26, we find David in his own Gethsemane moment. David and his men discover that Saul, who has been desperate to kill David, is vulnerable. David, or one of his men, could kill Saul and end the threat on David's life.

Abishai wrongly concludes that the Lord has led David to this moment to enact God's judgment against Saul. (As an aside, if we are looking for a way out of our hard place, we can usually find it and build a case to justify our behavior. Like Abishai, we can even wrongly conclude that this is God's will. We must be extremely, extremely cautious when using circumstance to decode the will of God. Scripture is the best teacher in that arena.) Further, Abishai offers to be Saul's executioner. Like Jesus in the Garden of Gethsemane, David halts the plan to take violent action.

You see, Abishai either didn't know or didn't understand God's command not to harm the Lord's anointed. David says that he will trust the judgment of Saul to the living God, saying "the LORD himself will strike him, or his time will come and he will die, or he will go into battle and perish" (1 Sam. 26:10).

Both David and Jesus refused to do what their followers wanted to do in favor of what would accomplish God's will. For David and Jesus, there was a potential solution that could have averted challenges in front of them—eliminating Saul and avoiding the cross. But David and Jesus didn't expect God to ease their suffering or change their circumstances for their conveniences. They didn't take the path of least resistance. They wouldn't opt for the easy way out. No, they trusted God to accomplish His will through them.

Remember that this is one of the major distinctions between self-help and sanctification.

You and I will inevitably face our own Gethsemane moments in life. Eventually we will face our own Abishai, a person who tempts us to do what's easy or quick. Those temptations are always there. The question is will we choose what is best over what is easiest? The Old and New Testaments affirm that God's purposes and God's glory rarely come easily.

God Is Best or God's Plan and Promises Are Best?

Throughout the hard season and real estate trial of 2008–2010, I had to choose to believe over and over again that God is better than anything I could hope for or imagine. And do you mind if I make what may seem like a kind of nit-picky point? It's not merely that *God's plan* is better than our plan. It's that God *Himself* is better than any other thing.

We have a habit of pinning our spiritual hopes on the promise that God has good things planned for us. I call it the Jeremiah 29:11 syndrome. Now, I love Jeremiah 29:11 as much as the next girl. I had an engraved picture frame with that verse on it in college. "'For I know the plans I have for you,'" declares the LORD, "'plans to prosper you and not to harm you, plans to give you hope and a future.'" I've clung to it through quite a few situations in the past. It's a good verse.

But it is a verse that was proclaimed over a people who were being promised a return to their land if they would return to the Lord. (And their return, as good a promise as it was, would take seventy years to fulfill!). The promise wasn't just about the land. The land always represented the promise and presence of God. Their hope and their future weren't tied just to their relationship with the land, but their relationship with their God.

God tells the prophet Jeremiah to make this grand pledge to Israel. God has a message for His wayward people. He makes good on His first promise of the land, but it means so, so much more than that. The Lord God makes a greater promise, a promise to be with His people in a personal, profound way. Look at what He has Jeremiah write regarding the New Covenant.

> "The days are coming," declares the LORD,
>   "when I will make a new covenant
> with the people of Israel
>   and with the people of Judah.
> It will not be like the covenant
>   I made with their ancestors
> when I took them by the hand
>   to lead them out of Egypt,
> because they broke my covenant,
>   though I was a husband to them,"
> declares the LORD.
> "This is the covenant I will make with the
>   people of Israel
>   after that time," declares the LORD.
> "I will put my law in their minds
>   and write it on their hearts.

I will be their God,
  and they will be my people.
No longer will they teach their neighbor,
  or say to one another, 'Know the LORD,'
because they will all know me,
  from the least of them to the greatest,"
declares the LORD.
"For I will forgive their wickedness
  and will remember their sins no more."
(Jer. 31:31–34)

But Israel misses the point. Even as they hear the promise, they don't fully understand it, nor commit their ways to the Lord. They understood what it meant to have the land, but to have the promise of God's presence? That was less clear. And let's be honest, less appealing. And when Jesus arrives on the scene, they hardly realize that He is the fulfillment of that New Covenant. We're not that different from Israel. We want the promises of God we can taste and see. Like Israel, we are a people more in love with the promises of God than the God of the promises.

> Like Israel, we are a people more in love with the promises of God than the God of the promises.

The grand story of Scripture isn't about stuff. It isn't a sweet life here. It's not even just an eternal life there. When we get to heaven we won't care how big our mansion is, what our new bodies look like, or whether or not we can shop, play baseball, or have pets. The greatest promise of Scripture is that God has a plan for a chosen people to enjoy Him forever. That's the point of heaven. Him. Him forever.

God calls His people to be separate. Separate is hard. Hard is good. But God is best. God is our treasure and portion. God is our highest aim and supreme joy. Our singular passion must be an intimate friendship with Him, or we miss the point.

The Process Is the Point

G od's presence and our joy in Him is the goal of life. Though it may seem like the neat-tidy, Sunday school answer, God really is the cure for my "me" sickness. Knowing that truth is one thing. Living that truth involves a whole lot of sanctification. And that sanctifying process takes us through seasons where God teaches us to live separate. He reminds us that separateness is hard, but if we will press through the hard places, we will discover that He is our best.

It is just that, a process.

A number of years ago my husband and I watched dear friends deal with soul-crushing suffering. We were invited into their pain and had a front row seat to watch them grieve, cope, grieve some more, and by God's grace, heal.

The experience of sanctification isn't the same for everyone. It's deeply personal, and different from person to person and situation to situation. But the consistent part of it all is that, again, *it's a process.*

Whenever I need to be reminded of those lessons of suffering, I go back and read Job. Throughout the book, as we've discussed previously, Job and his friends ping-pong arguments back and forth. There is a process to his pain, and where he lands in Job 13 is both hopeful and heartbreaking.

Isn't that life? Sorrow, anger, frustration, or hurt comes in waves and makes everything feel uncertain. One minute we are confident. The next minute we are caught in a riptide of doubt and fear. Yet in the midst of Job's confusion, he clings to God's character. As we read through Job's replies, look for what he says about God.

Throughout his rebuttals in Job chapters 6, 9, 10, and 12, Job extols the attributes and character of God. Here are a few of the things Job says:

> God is worthy of loyalty and faith.
>
> God is the righteous judge.
>
> God is the answer-giver.
>
> God alone has wisdom, might, counsel, and understanding.

It is Job's faith in God that leads him to say his famous words in chapter 13 that even if God would slay Job, he will still hope in God. Job's confidence in God's righteous judgment leads Job to conclude he will see God face-to-face. Job is convinced of his integrity before the Lord, and only the upright stand before God. Chapter 13 is a heartbreaking highlight for Job.

> "Though he slay me, yet will I hope in him; I will surely defend my ways to his face. Indeed, this will turn out for my deliverance, for no godless person would dare come before him!" (Job 13:15–16)

Despite his friends' accusations, Job has wrestled well with the grief and pain of suffering. He doesn't have answers, but Job trusts what he doesn't know to the One who knows all. I love that each chapter shows Job in a real and raw way, trying to reconcile his emotions with the truth of who God is.

Knowing who God is doesn't necessarily change Job's circumstances or ours. Life isn't easy, and every question doesn't have an easy answer. But the process is part of the point. And I'm grateful that the book of Job gives us an example of what that messy, hard process looks like.

What we've discovered up to this point is that God is doing a work in us. He intends to make us like Christ. He isn't trying to help us live our best life by the world's standards. He isn't making our lives tidy or comfortable. In Romans 8:28, He promises He is working all things together for our good. For those of us who are called according to His purposes, we can have confidence that it's all going to work out okay, right?

Well, if one of the first goals of this book is to help us understand the process of sanctification, then a secondary goal of the book is to rescue verses that have been ripped out of context and slapped on situations that may not be fair. Romans 8:28, like Jeremiah 29:11, is one of those verses.

Yes, God will work all things for good for those who are called according to His purposes. But what is His chief purpose for His children? To make us more like Christ. Why do I think that? Because that's what Romans 8:29–30 says. Check it out.

> For those God foreknew he also predestined to be conformed to the image of his Son, that he might be the firstborn among many brothers and sisters. And those he predestined, he also called; those he called, he also justified; those he justified, he also glorified.

Everything God is doing in us (calling, justifying, and glorifying) is to transform us into the image of His Son. God is working all things out for our good *according to His purpose* (not our own). In other words, He's working all things to make you and me more like Jesus. You guys, that's so different than how I've typically used Romans 8:28 as a Band-Aid verse. I've tried to use that verse to promise somebody in pain that it will get better. That God will bring good from this horrible situation. That's true, but I'm usually picturing the kind of "good" I think God means.

When a friend had a miscarriage, I sent her this verse. So many of you reading this right now have suffered the unique and debilitating pain of miscarriage. I am so, so sorry. I'd say to you what I wished I'd said to my friend. I'm sorry, and your pain is real, valuable, and completely okay. Your grief isn't less. It's not silly. And you mourn in any way and for as long as you need. Nothing will replace or fix that loss. Forgive me, forgive all of us, who said something foolish when we should have just said nothing.

Could Romans 8:28 bring her comfort? Without question. This verse is written into a passage where Paul is trying to comfort those who are suffering. But if I'm honest, what I wanted this verse to say, what I was trying to say to my dear, grieving friend is this:

> "God will bring good from your pain. Something better. Something purposeful. You'll be happy, I promise. You'll look back on this and know exactly what He was doing and why. Take hope. God won't let you hurt forever. This will be a good thing down the road."

Do you see how this kind of hope isn't what Paul was talking about? Do you see how this kind of hope can actually undercut our faith and purpose of suffering? Any mom who's had a miscarriage can tell you that it often doesn't seem to have a purpose. Even if God is gracious enough to create life again and that baby is born healthy and happy, it doesn't diminish the pain of his or her sibling not being there to celebrate. And the reality is, we probably won't ever understand why. And for sure, Mom who's mourned, you won't be happy about it down the road. Can you make peace with God's will? Yes. But does the pain go away? My friend who's been there says "no." Now when I engage a friend in a painful situation, I don't use Romans 8 to promise her that the situation will eventually shape up. I promise her what that passage is actually saying: that somehow, some way, God is using this suffering to shape *her* up into the image of His Son. This *will* make her more like Christ. That she can bank on.

That's why Romans 8:28 isn't meant to be a filter for our circumstances. It's meant to be a frame for what God is doing in us. And here's an important shift. Everything God is doing in our lives is about Christ in us. Suffering may not be about me, but it is meant to change me.

This shift takes suffering and hard sessions from torture or tribulation to transformation. This isn't something that is just happening to me; this is something that is happening for me. Do our circumstances stink? Is grief gut-wrenching? Is life not fair? Yes, yes, a thousand times, yes. But is there a purpose in all of it? To that I say a good, Southern amen.

The process isn't pointing me toward better circumstances, but toward something and Someone. I am changing not to be in a better situation, but to be like *Christ*.

Whose Process?

Like many newlyweds at our wedding reception, Chad and I had a traditional first dance. Now it wasn't the stuff of epic, viral first dances. Nope. It was a rather boring demonstration. Very, very vanilla. We treated our guests to several minutes of us recycling the same three moves and shuffling around to Etta James's "At Last." Oh, and there was one fairly awkward dip at the end. One dip. And we nearly fell over.

When I was in college, I made a list of all the things I prayed to find in a husband. And ladies, I was ambitious. Forty-two qualifications, to be exact. I wanted my future husband to be my spiritual leader, have dark hair, be a hard worker, love kids, and think I was beautiful. These were just a few qualities of my ridiculously specific list. Also on the list? I wanted my husband to love to dance. Chad and I have been married a long time. And I can tell you that he meets or exceeds every requirement on my list except that one. But in all our years of marriage, I've never, ever thought, *Man, I wish I'd waited for a man who can dance.* Yes, I compromised. Yet, Chad is still so much better than anything I could have dreamed or described. But is he a dancer? That would be a categorical "no."

I'm not much of a dancer either, but I can follow a strong partner. Chad is the most exceptional leader I've ever seen. In business, he is thoughtful, decisive, collaborative, and confident. But on the dance floor, well, he's the exact opposite of all that. So, during our wedding dance, I tried to lead, but we ended up stepping on one another's toes. A lot. When that didn't work, I tried to coach him along. I'd whisper in his ear what next steps to take, so I could "follow" him. That way it would look like he was leading, but I was still in charge, making sure we didn't do something that would haunt us for the rest of our lives. This thing was being videoed after all! That didn't work either. In dancing you're not really leading if you have to be told what to do.

On that May evening in 2001, we moved around to music, but I don't know that legit dancers would say we "danced." We were going through the motions, but we weren't dancing.

When I look back on my spiritual journey—the dance I have with the Lord—I'd say the same has been true. I've been going through the motions, but I don't know if you'd call it dancing. I've often thought that I know the song better. Or I've danced along to a song in my head, trying to make my own music. Sometimes I would break dance when the Lord was trying to lead me to waltz. I resisted the gentle pull of His arms, pushing Him away so I could do my own thing.

> Sanctification is *God's* process to lead.

Now in this analogy, God is nothing like my Chad (when it comes to dancing). Our strong and tender God is completely competent to lead us. He knows all the moves to take. He knows the rhythm of our life perfectly; He wrote the music. He isn't making it up as He goes along. It's all been perfectly orchestrated since the beginning of time. At the end of the day, this dance of sanctification is *God's* process to lead. He's the one who has designed it. He's the one in control of it. He's the one setting the pace. At the end of your faith journey, you *will* be sanctified because God is the one initiating the whole thing, and He promises to finish the dances that He starts.

81

Pursuing the Process, Part 1: Confident and Unashamed

Yes, the dance of sanctification is *God's* to lead. It's *His* process. But even the strongest partner can't lead if His partner won't follow.

And friend, I'm not great at following. How about you?

Here's the real tension. Sanctification isn't a solo. The process God uses to make us more holy is like taking dance class. We may know the steps, but that doesn't make us a dancer. Some of us have learned the moves, but we get on the floor and freestyle. Some of us want to learn by watching. I'm reminded of an episode of *Friends* where Monica, Phoebe, and Rachel go to a tap class. (It's the episode where a girl has stolen Monica's identity.) They arrive at the class and tell the instructor they just want to observe. She dramatically responds, "You don't watch a dance class; you dance a dance class."

You guys, we weren't made to dance alone, and we weren't made to simply observe. We were made to dance with Jesus. That's the process. Will we step on His toes from time to time? Sure. Will we pull away, turn the wrong direction, or get it wrong? Probably often. But that's the gig. We keep dancing. And over time, we will learn how to follow. We will see the patterns in the moves. We will start to get the "feel" for how He guides us.

And eventually, we will find the rhythm that doesn't feel at all like work.

Remember our primary definition of sanctification—it's *both the divine process and the human pursuit of being made into the image of Christ.* Up to this point we have been talking about the divine process of becoming more like Christ, the way He leads the dance. As we think about our being separate and being satisfied in God, most of what we have discussed has revolved around our passive response to the work of God in our lives. He calls us out. He invites us into hard places to prove to us the worthlessness of other passions and the great worth of knowing Jesus Christ. In living through seasons of suffering we discover that God is trustworthy and our best hope for happiness. And through it all, He is making us more holy. This is the divine process of sanctification.

But as we've said, sanctification is both a divine process (God's part) *and* a human pursuit (our part). For those of us who are anxious to do something and love a good to-do list, this is for us. Because yes, we are to take an active part in the pursuit of growing in Christlikeness. We have a part to play in the dance.

Can I lean in though, and give you and me both a caveat? Remember my story about my porch flowers and the repotting? It is our tendency to focus on the exterior, do our part, and allow ourselves and others to be distracted by what appears to be growth. But even now that we know the ways God works in us to make us more holy, let's not rush past our submission to it. This next part won't ever be fruitful if we're still root-bound in our old pots.

If there is good news in being root-bound, it is this. We are in good company. I wonder if the apostle Paul would have described the Philippians this way. He certainly wanted more for his beloved church family of Philippi. Philippians is Paul's letter of exhortation and appreciation to his friends. With Timothy's help, Paul expresses his gratitude for their prayers and financial support. Don't you love a kind word of encouragement? Right when I need it the most, sometimes I'll receive a handwritten note, or my phone alerts me of a text message saying, "I prayed for you today." The leaders at Philippi must have felt loved as they read Paul's letter to their church.

It's important to note that Paul is writing this letter of encouragement from prison. Paul was arrested for preaching the gospel (Acts 25). I find this amazing! In a place where he himself needed encouragement, Paul offered encouragement to others. Paul's situation should challenge us. When we are in a prison of sorts, be it physically, financially, or emotionally, we can look not to what is happening to us, but what is happening through us.

Hard circumstances like Paul faced, and like we face, are the substance of God's growth for the believer. In fact, this is one of the major themes of Philippians: God is sanctifying or maturing us through suffering. The good work God has begun in you, He will complete. God's end goal is His own glory, and God is glorified when His children grow to be like Him!

God begins this good work, and He is faithful to complete it. But what did God start? God began His work in the hearts of individual believers in Philippi. Philippi is the first place in Europe where the gospel was preached. When Paul and Silas went to Macedonia to share the gospel with the Gentiles, Philippi was their first stop. This group of believers to whom Paul is writing was the first church in Macedonia. Because of their love for God and their "partnership in the gospel," they have been sending him aid while he was imprisoned in Rome. God began the work, but they have followed in obedience.

This is a good word for you and me. Most of us are probably beginning to see our present circumstances in a new way. Perhaps you are beginning to see that God is calling you out of something familiar. Maybe He's inviting you to a new place or giving you a new purpose. Or it's possible, that like me, you are in a season of hardship and God is re-framing all the pain so that you see it as a promise of His faithfulness. And maybe, just maybe, we are beginning to see that God is, in fact, our best.

But no matter where we are, it's still likely that the process isn't over. In fact, if you're breathing, I can guarantee you it's not. But what do we do in the middle of a process? How do we live in between the beginning of the good work and its completion? We do what the Philippians did. We stay present in the present.

In the in-between time there are lessons to be learned, experiences to be had, and faithfulness to be lived. Staying present in the present means we fiercely study God's Word, pray fervently, and obey everything God asks us to do. The time in between prepares us for what He has already prepared for us "for we are God's handiwork, created in Christ Jesus to do good works, which God prepared in advance for us to do" (Eph. 2:10).

This is sanctification, and God will one day complete that process for you and me. The day we see Jesus face-to-face, He will say to us, "It is finished." The tension that you and I are living in is that while Jesus has certainly said, "It is finished," if you have breath in your body He hasn't said, "*You* are finished." Jesus has finished the work of the cross. He has finished the work that made us right before God. Jesus has justified us. But He is not done sanctifying us. He still has those "good works" for us to do.

There is this part of sanctification that is a pursuit. Remember we've said that sanctification is a process where we partner with God. We respond to the process that He's working out in us by obediently pursuing Him.

And now, all my type-A, hyper-focused, let's-get-it-done girls are saying, "But how?" Am I right? Girl, me too. Because yes, I want to let God work in me. Yes, I want to see my circumstances and hard seasons with one eye on me and one eye on Jesus. But yes, I also want to do my part. And while both are always happening simultaneously, let's move from looking at the process, to learning about the pursuit.

Let's do this.

Confident and Unashamed

So what does sanctification look like? What is the *goal* that we are shooting for? Well, remember that complete sanctification doesn't happen until we see Jesus face-to-face. But John provides a description that I think helps give us a goal to shoot for. In 1 John 2:28 he says, "And now, dear children, continue in him, so that when he appears we may be confident and unashamed before him at his coming."

"Confident and unashamed." Isn't that a lovely description? Oh friend, when I see Jesus, that's exactly how I'd like to be. Confident and unashamed. Though my greeting Jesus feels far away most days, I still wonder if I'll be ready. How does one become confident and unashamed? How do we get from where we are now to where we want to be in the end when we see Jesus? Because goodness, I'd like to be confident and unashamed now, or at least on my way.

First John 2 gives us a way of pursuing the confident, unashamed life. For those of us who read Scripture and think, *Just tell me what to do, and I'll do it*, this is for you. John gives us some really practical things to consider in the pursuit of sanctification.

Sanctification is how the Holy Spirit works within us to make us more like Christ. Historically, sanctification has been described in two ways—progressive and definitive. When we profess faith in Christ, He makes us holy and righteous before God. This can also be called justification or definitive sanctification, and we've already discussed what that means. The definition of progressive sanctification, on the other hand, is what we've been talking about all along: the divine process and the human pursuit of us being crucified and conformed to the image of Christ.

Sanctification is a beautiful thing where God works in us, and we respond to His extravagant grace with obedience. Our part in that process seems to be what John is describing here. Like the work of sanctification itself, this chapter is a progression. It gives us the language to define what the sanctified life looks like.

I'm the type of person who gets easily overwhelmed. It's yet another way that my husband Chad and I are completely different. The bigger, the more challenging the problem, the more motivated Chad is to beat it. For me, the bigger the problem, the bigger the procrastination. Complicated, undefined tasks seem impossible to me. I need to see where I'm going and then have small, manageable tasks to get there.

Throughout 1 John 2, we get those small, manageable tasks. But for now, let's just focus on the endgame—being women who are confident and unashamed.

Who do you picture when you think about a confident woman? For me, she's part beauty queen (likely in the swimsuit portion of the competition) and part glammed-up, Oscar-winning actress. She's a glowing Jennifer Aniston. But I'm not sure that's what John is getting at. Clearly, he wasn't thinking beauty queen or Hollywood actress, but I don't think he was even imagining the ancient Near Eastern version, like a dolled-up Cleopatra or Jezebel. Not likely.

But even if I could imagine some other "confident" woman, I can't imagine that woman ever being me. Do you feel the same way? In Christian circles, confident is the sister of a less-esteemed emotion called "pride." Of all the things I want to be when I face Jesus, or live among His people here, prideful is at the bottom of that list. But you see that's not what John is getting at here. This is where studying the original language helps iron out the wrinkles of our misinterpretation.

The word used here in 1 John 2:28 is used elsewhere in Scripture. The uses of the word typically fall into two categories—speech and faith. In *Thayer's Greek Lexicon*, the word has two descriptive definitions: "freedom in speaking, unreserved in speech" or "free and fearless confidence, cheerful courage." The summary of biblical usage includes speaking frankly, without ambiguity; free and fearless; assured. Yes, I'd like a biggie size order of that.

Passages like John 16:25 and Acts 2:29 address how Jesus and Peter, like others in Scripture, speak with clarity, boldness, and confidence about God and His kingdom. We'd say they don't mince words or sugarcoat the truth. This is one meaning of the Greek word *confident.*

89

But biblical confidence isn't limited to what we say. In fact, confident words are the fruit of confident faith. The second definition communicates that we have cheerful courage, that we are free and fearless. Consider Ephesians 3:12: "In him and through faith in him we may approach God with freedom and confidence." The "him" in that passage is Jesus Christ. Because of Jesus, we approach God with confidence. Even more so, the point of this particular portion of the letter to the Ephesians is that because of Jesus, God is welcoming Gentiles into His family. The Gentile believers were often ostracized or ridiculed because they didn't have a backstory like the Jewish believers. They were the outsiders, the rarely confident ones. And yet, it's to these believers that Paul is writing. He wants confidence for those who usually aren't.

> **Confident words are the fruit of confident faith.**

Confidence for the less-than-confident. Yep. That's me. How about you? Ever felt on the outside? Good news. Confidence isn't based on being a part of the cool kids. Maybe you've been embarrassed by your background. You're in luck. Confidence isn't dependent on what all you know. Our confidence comes *from* Christ. And our confidence is *in Christ.*

You see, friend, our confidence isn't in ourselves but rather in the Lord Jesus Christ. Christ-confident people don't carry shame from their past. Christ-confident people don't get hung up on their own inadequacies. Christ-confident people don't look to others to determine their own worth. We have no need to build our trust in who we are or have been. It's only Jesus.

When we get a taste of that kind of Christ-confidence, we can't help but share it. That kind of confidence is contagious. Can you remember a time that you felt that way? The stuff of your faith felt so real that you almost couldn't keep it in? I haven't felt that often, but when I have felt that way I remember not being consumed with what other people thought of me. I remember being completely consumed with Jesus and pleasing Him.

That's the substance of the confidence to which John is referring.

Now perhaps you can wrap your brain around confidence. Maybe being completely consumed with Jesus and what He has done sounds really nice. But to live unashamed? Well that one is a little trickier.

Living a life unashamed is harder to grab ahold of. I mean, live confident in the work of Jesus? I get that. Forget the mountain of debt I had against God? Live completely free from the guilt and shame of that? So much harder, right? Shame is a stubborn weed that comes back no matter how many times I pull it, you know?

When the devil begins to attack us, it's best not to argue with him. I've lost quite a few arguments with the devil. I know I have authority over him, but when he starts reading my rap sheet of crimes against God and comparing me to other women, I can get sucked into a "me" spiral. When this starts to happen, the only solution is to take *me* out of the equation. The only way to shut up the devil is at the cross.

The church at Colossae knew about having an attacked, vulnerable faith. One of the purposes of Paul's letter to the Colossians was to firm up their faith and remind them of their confidence in the cross. In Colossians 2:14–15 Paul says, "Having canceled the charge of our legal indebtedness, which stood against us and condemned us; he has taken it away, nailing it to the cross. And having disarmed the powers and authorities, he made a public spectacle of them, triumphing over them by the cross."

In the Ancient Near East, agreements and business transactions between two parties were handwritten into formal contracts—not unlike today, but with a few more ink strokes rather than keystrokes. When one party was indebted to another, his name would be written below the agreement. When the debt was satisfied, the name would be scratched out, a line drawn through it, or one would hammer a nail, piercing the name, signifying the debt had been canceled.

The only way to shut up the devil is at the cross.

In Colossians 2, Paul uses this same idea with the phrase "legal indebtedness." The law of God was the written contract that held us in debt to Him. Sins stacked up, and our charges against Him were incalculable. But through Jesus Christ, God has canceled those charges!

Because of the very specific word choice Paul used in verse 14, his audience would have envisioned the nails in Jesus' hands and feet blotting out the debt we owed God. Every charge against us was nailed to the cross. Our account with Him had been settled. He can forgive us because even though we failed to uphold our end of the contract by keeping the law, Jesus paid the price for our crimes against God. We were unable to meet the terms of our agreement with Him. So Jesus did that for us by living a perfect, completely sinless life and taking on the shame of our sin by dying a criminal's death in our place. This is referred to by scholars as *expiation*. To "expiate" our sin means that Jesus satisfied the legal requirements that God demands of us.

This is the gospel. Our debt is paid! The nails that pierced Him declared us free and clear. What marvelous news! It's a sweet reminder to combat our shame and guilt. The cross is the antidote. The cross sets us free from shame.

But living unashamed isn't just forgetting what we've done. Sometimes we also have to let go of all the stuff we *haven't* done. For some of us, we live in a state of constant comparison wondering why we don't measure up to "her." Whose Instagram account do you check out but end up feeling worse about yourself? Is there a woman that you look at and think, *I just don't know how she does it*? Now, you are probably much more emotionally healthy than I am. But I don't stop there. I don't just wonder how she does it, but I then wonder why I can't. Comparison brings its own brand of shame.

Here's my own brand of crazy. I love to read. It's one of my favorite things. (And moms whose kids don't read, and you're sure you've failed, take heart. I never read as a kid. Cut yourself some slack. You're not a failure if your kid never turns into a bibliophile.) But in the process of writing this book, I had to stop reading. That seems really, really counterintuitive, right? But you see I struggle with the shame that comes from comparison. I was reading countless books by female authors, and all I could think were things like,

> *She's so much smarter than me. Why am I doing this?*

Sick of Me

She's already taught something kind of like what I'm teaching, and it's really, really good. Women would probably prefer to read her book.

She is so much more accomplished. Why would God use me?

The devil is one sneaky sucker. I'd spend days trying to bounce back and find my writing mojo. I'd pray and pray, but sometimes even prayer wasn't enough. The shame, over all the things I lack and all the things I hadn't done, was nearly suffocating. Insecurity crippled me. Like we said before, there's a void. This kind of void is meant to teach us something about God, to be filled with something eternal and holy. But when there is a gap, I am desperate to fill it.

The temptation is for us to look for acceptance of who we are and affirmation of what God has called us to do. But that's another pitfall altogether.

Not long ago, I sat in a theater where I didn't know anyone except my date and husband (the same dude by the way), but roughly a hundred people were connected and captivated in an instant by *The Greatest Showman*. The movie opens with a silhouetted man dancing to the music, twirling his hat, and clicking his cane to the beat. Seconds later the screen was alive with color, music, and vocalists awakening every movie-goer to the joy and beauty of song. I didn't know the tune, but my foot tapped along to a rhythm I seemed to know even though I'd never heard it before. There was a universal anticipation in that theater.

If you haven't seen it already, I highly recommend you spend a couple hours being entertained by the staggering talent of Hugh Jackman, the previously unknown Keala Settle, and special talents of Zendaya and Zac Efron, yes, of *High School Musical* fame. Untainted by crass language or overt, unnecessary sexuality, *The Greatest Showman* is a wonderful story about passion, vision, and acceptance. I was swept up in the mostly fictional story of Phineas Taylor Barnum. It was like "dreaming with your eyes wide open" (a line from one of the intoxicating anthems of the first act).

I won't spoil it for you, but the movie's characters at one point thank P. T. for giving them a home and making them a family. These misfits had been left out of society, excluded and ridiculed for not being "normal." Their collective dysfunctions and abnormalities made them a circus congregation. They found something together each had always been looking for—acceptance.

Inclusion and self-acceptance are major themes of *The Greatest Showman.* The words have been so overplayed and politicized that it's easy to bristle at the idea, wondering what agenda is being pushed. But friend, these ideals like so many have been co-opted by the culture. In actuality each are ideas—virtues even—that originated with our virtuous God. All virtues find their source in Him. There isn't beauty apart from Him. There isn't goodness apart from Him. The concepts of inclusion and acceptance find their grounding, or right and basic understanding, in God.

The Greatest Showman is beautifully gospel-close, but not gospel-centered. Like most things that our culture appropriates, there is Truth here, but the movie stops short, missing the ultimate hope we have in Jesus. It's not surprising, but it is an opportunity.

People desperately want acceptance. People are lonely and want to feel included. People want to be connected and known. And you know what? I am "people." I have felt all of these things. Still do. How about you? What a beautiful bridge to our lost neighbors, lonely coworkers, hurting and broken friends. We can say to them, "We get it; we understand."

This movie celebrates a premature and temporal resolution. It's the best the writers, producers, and actors could do apart from Jesus. It's a fine way to end a movie; it's a terrible way to end a life. Because, friend, people aren't just in need of a community, family, or home here. Much, much more is at stake and available.

But these impulses are meant to be experienced and viewed in light of the cross. The gospel is most centrally a change-agent. The gospel says, "Come just as you are." Then the gospel follows with, "But you cannot stay that way." There isn't inclusion except through the available-to-all grace of Jesus Christ. That's our unifying battle cry. Cross-acceptance is the endgame.

Self-acceptance? That's a different conversation all together. Self-acceptance is the beginning of self-denial. For the believer, accepting who we are isn't the same thing as affirming who we are. I can tell you that there is little to celebrate in me apart from Christ.

Our friends, family members, neighbors, coworkers, and fellow students don't need a Hollywood ending. They need a Jesus beginning.

When we think about living a life that is unashamed, don't confuse that ideal with acceptance. That's not what John was describing. And affirming or applauding who we are outside of

God has never been a call of the gospel. There is more, so much more, to celebrate. There is Someone who wants to fill every vacancy and inadequacy we have. It's been His plan from the very beginning.

Where Moses Finds Confidence and Affirmation

I love, love, love Moses. He's one of my favorite Bible leads. He was the baby in the basket put in the Nile to save him from the mandated infanticide of jealous Pharaoh. The Hebrew slave nation was growing too big to control so Pharaoh ordered that all male babies be killed. Pharaoh's daughter plucks Moses from the Nile and raises him as Egyptian royalty.

Moses lives in the castle, is educated by the best tutors, learns the Egyptian language and culture. But for Moses it must have been obvious that he wasn't one of them. He was on the outside even inside the castle, I suspect. Moses, like many of us, had a space of insecurity that nothing could fill. Not wealth. Not power. Not the fake gods of Egypt. In Exodus 2 the Bible records that Moses saw an Egyptian beating a Hebrew and Moses felt compelled to defend the Hebrew because "he was one of his people." Insecurity will beg us to fill the void. We will strive to prove that insecurity is a liar. But striving is rarely successful. Ask Moses.

He kills the Egyptian beating his Hebrew brother and buries the body to keep it a secret. But Moses' secret doesn't stay buried. What he did is discovered, and Moses is forced to flee to the Midian desert to avoid Pharaoh's efforts to kill him.

In the desert Moses begins work as a shepherd. God has gotten Moses alone. In his desert wandering, in the third chapter of

Exodus, we will see a man wrestle with God about two of life's great questions.

"Who am I?"

"Who is God?"

In Exodus 3:14, "God said to Moses, 'I AM WHO I AM. This is what you are to say to the Israelites: 'I AM has sent me to you.'"

In a burning bush encounter, God calls Moses away from the busyness of life to encounter the presence of the living God in a profound and personal way. Moses has been living in Midian for about forty years. God explains that in this wilderness He has been silently preparing Moses to shepherd the Hebrew slaves to freedom.

Moses was to go and demand that Pharaoh let God's people go. Moses' response is, "Who am I that I should go?" (v. 11).

Moses has been in exile hiding from Pharaoh for forty years. Now God wants him to return. No doubt this former man-of-action has had his confidence shaken. He probably felt like a forgotten failure. This is an important reminder for us. We are never forgotten in the wilderness of our lives. God is often preparing our character to match our calling.

Moses left Egypt a prince. He had been educated, reared, and trained to know Egypt, lead people, and defend a nation. Perhaps Moses asked this question hoping God would recite this résumé back to Moses. Like Moses, when God has given me a spiritual assignment, I hope He'll also give me confidence in my skill and preparation to make saying "yes" a bit easier. Have you been there? God asks you to do something that you really, really feel ill-equipped to do. Or maybe you think that possibly, you have some skill, but wonder if it's enough—if you're enough—for what the Lord is asking you to do.

When God called me into ministry, I was at this women's conference listening to this woman open God's Word and teach it with passion, clarity, and joy. In that moment, I sensed in some way that God might want me to do something similar with my life. I remember exactly where I was sitting. I remember what I was wearing. (It was a red twin set from Ann Taylor and a pair of high-waisted, wide-leg jeans from Gap. And I had on a brown braided belt and brown platform shoes. It was so 1997.)

I felt so overwhelmed at the thought that God would use me that I immediately began asking Him to convince me that He could use me and to prove that I heard Him right. Like Moses, I thought, *Who am I that You would use me?* I'm not proud of it, but rather than asking Him to build my faith up, I wanted Him to build me up.

That's not how God responds—to Moses or to me or to you.

More than any person in history, Moses was equipped for God's assignment. But God used forty years of wilderness wandering to strip Moses of his self-confidence. He didn't need Moses' qualifications, and He doesn't need ours.

God doesn't build Moses up. No. Don't miss verse 12. God simply says that He's going with Moses. When God wants to give us confidence, He doesn't applaud our gifts. He promises His presence. How God answers Moses reminds us that who we are isn't nearly as important as who He is. Friend, when God wants to use us, He rarely affirms us; He always affirms Himself.

Are you waiting to feel qualified before you say "yes" to that thing God is asking you to do? Does He want you to start that non-profit? Has He asked you to take over that ministry? Maybe

He keeps harassing you to reach out to that lonely neighbor or fix that broken relationship. He can be so relentless, right? If you're waiting to feel good enough, I'm not sure you'll step into obedience. If you can find a place in Scripture where God builds up the person He's called, please tell me. I've looked. It seems that rather than affirming the person He's called, God almost always affirms Himself.

Those voids in our capabilities? God wants to fill them with His sufficiency, not our striving. But this isn't the end of Moses' conversation with God.

Moses asks God for a bit more clarity. He wants to know God's Name. Who is this One who promises to be with Moses?

> It seems that rather than affirming the person He's called, God almost always affirms Himself.

Up to this point in Scripture God has only identified Himself with one name: El Shaddai. In Genesis 17:1, God introduced Himself to Abraham as El Shaddai, "God Almighty."

Generations of Hebrew families had worshipped their God as El Shaddai. It's possible that this is the name Moses expected God to use. But God has a special assignment for Moses and it comes with a special revelation about God Himself.

God answers in Exodus 3:14, "I AM WHO I AM." This is His Name, "Yahweh." Scholars wrestle with an exact translation and meaning of this introduction. One possible meaning is, "I will be to you ALL that I AM." I love that. The patriarchs of the faith knew God by a part of His indescribable character. Now God promises His presence by revealing that He will be everything that Moses and Israel will ever need.

This is huge. It's not that He will *provide* everything they need, though He will certainly do that. It's that *He* is everything they need. *The provision is tied to His very presence!*

His almighty power of deliverance.

His miraculous control over nature and creation.

His divine protection through the desert.

All of His majestic glory would be on display and available to them because He is their ALL. Moses didn't get a demonstration of God's might; he was promised God's very being.

"I AM."

Do you respond to God's invitations in your life waiting to feel self-confident and affirmed? As John and Moses teach us, that's completely different from the call to live confident and unashamed. Is your faith based on who you are, how faithful you have been, or could be? Or is it anchored in the presence of God and His profoundly sufficient character? Yes, who we are isn't nearly as important as who He is.

Living confident and unashamed are the liberating fruit of a life that is consumed with Christ. We are free from the pressure of others' expectations and unchained from the fear of our own inadequacy because Jesus has made us righteous and God has promised to go with us wherever He calls us. Instead of self-confident, we're *God*-confident. Instead of desperately needing affirmation that we are enough, we are affirmed that *God* is enough.

Easy to say. Hard to live.

Thankfully John gives us some practical help in this area. As I said, John encourages us to live confident and unashamed as the endgame. But the chapter actually offers some helpful and practical ways to pursue that kind of holiness, as we will explore in the next chapter.

Pursuing the Process, Part 2: Our Part

God's Word gives us the *goal* of living confident and unashamed, yes, but it doesn't leave the goal hanging out there, unattainable for us. What's beautiful about this passage in 1 John 2 is that it also outlines the *steps* toward that goal. It helps us see our part in God's process.

John's first admonition is that we do not sin and that we keep God's commands. I think it's interesting that John ties *confession* with *obedience*. I was really, really convicted by this passage. I think sometimes I try to skip the confession part and skip right to the obedience part.

But confession primes our hearts to pursue obedience. We can't change what we won't admit, remember? More often than not my confession of sin is a kind of basic catch-all, "forgive me where I've failed today" situation. As we've said, generic confession leads to generic obedience. But when we ask God to forgive us for, let's say, giving into the gossip our friends were exchanging, you can bet that the next time we begin to fall into the same pattern, God's Holy Spirit will bring it to our attention. It's hard to ignore conviction for something so specific.

Paying attention to sin helps us invest our efforts in the best places to see change. But if we're honest, most of us would rather ignore sin. But sin is a cancer. It can't kill the believer, but it can make our life painful, tiresome, and lonely. So how do we pay attention to sin? What steps can we take to lessen its hold on our lives?

Confession and Obedience

I love the book of Leviticus. I avoided it for so long. But once I really studied it, I've come to the conclusion that I could use a little more Leviticus in my life.

One of the passages that I came to love was actually about boils and skin diseases. What? I know, right? But stay with me. Leviticus 13:46 says, "As long as they have the disease they remain unclean. They must live alone; they must live outside the camp."

This section of Leviticus outlines the contaminating effects of skin diseases. For Israel, leaving an invasive, contagious disease unchecked meant endangering the entire nation. Skin diseases could spread with catastrophic consequence.

Here we see that the priests were entrusted not just with the spiritual health of the people but their physical health as well. God takes great lengths to train the priests and define the diseases that threatened Israel.

It may not be enjoyable to read about swelling, scabs, and sores, but remember that God has a plan that is bigger than just the spread of disease.

Certainly it was possible for this ever-faithful God to protect them from disease in the first place. That would be much easier than teaching them to inspect these skin sores. But easiness rarely leads to holiness.

There is a more important lesson for them and for us. Teaching them to be attentive to the potential threat of spreading contagions reminds them of a greater spiritual lesson—sin spreads and corrupts if left unchecked. God wanted His people to vigilantly protect themselves against the spread of sin. He didn't want them overlooking its initial symptoms and underestimating its devastating appetite.

The priests were not just to acknowledge the presence of a threat, but also to deal with it quickly and decisively. Those who were under observation were placed in isolation outside the camp. Their condition was to be named and acknowledged by the whole community.

This may seem unnecessarily harsh to you and me. But God is never unnecessarily harsh. When our belief about God is in conflict with the rest of Scripture, we need to reevaluate our conclusion.

Our discomfort is not a reflection on the character of our loving and tender God. Our discomfort is a reflection on us. Do we want to allow for small sins or excuse "innocent" offenses? God communicated in no uncertain terms the threat complacency posed to the community. And just like those in Leviticus, we are at risk when we overlook or underestimate the real power sin has to spread if it's not named, acknowledged, and dealt with, not just by us, but in community.

I love Leviticus, and its theme—calling God's people to holiness—steps on my toes. Sin spreads, corrupts, and devastates. God takes it seriously. So should we. But maybe talking sores, boils, and mold seems unrelatable. Let me help make it more contemporary.

Studying, meditating, and memorizing God's Word is a beautiful "both/and" as it relates to confession. Scripture is the mirror that God uses to point out the blemishes in my life. For years I have prayed that the boys would be just like Chad in almost every regard. His smarts. His looks. His winsome personality. His work ethic. But I have always prayed that my boys would have my teeth, my eyes, and my skin. I was the rare teenager who escaped the awkward phase of braces, glasses, or zits. "Oh the overwhelming, never-ending reckless love of God."

But one time when I was in the seventh grade, I sat down at the lunch table and one of my friends said, "Oh my gosh, you have a massive zit on your chin! I've never seen you with a pimple. Hey everybody, Whitney has a pimple!" And I'm not exaggerating when I say she was literally pointing from across the table at my chin. I was mortified.

Now in seventh grade, I didn't wear makeup or do a lot with my hair. That particular day I had just thrown it in a ponytail. I don't think I'd even looked in a mirror that morning. Now it was lunch, halfway through my day, and Ashley had just announced to the entire table that I had an obvious zit on my chin. Awesome.

I scurried to the bathroom with my hand over my chin, only to find that Ashley was right, and she wasn't being dramatic. In fact, she may have been gracious. Y'all! This thing needed its own zip code or locker. I could have died.

In that moment I promised myself that I'd never go to school again without checking in the mirror first.

Far worse than an untimely, unfortunate pimple, Scripture saves us from stepping out into the world with the blemishes of jealousy, bitterness, gossip, anger, laziness, gluttony, or pride. When I spend time in God's Word, I see Jesus and, mercifully, I see myself. His Word helps me see the areas that need cleansing. And I am so grateful, not because my spotless skin matters, but because I'm reflecting His unblemished character. Those boils, sores, and diseases we talked about earlier were an ancient mirror of sorts. God was training them like He trains us today. We must look out for the blemishes in our lives, and Scripture is the perfect mirror for that kind of self-examination.

(As an aside, no book is a replacement for His Book. Certainly not mine, but authors far smarter than me are still a pitiful substitute. Have you ever tried to style, braid, or fix the back of your hair using a mirror to look in a mirror? It's crazy hard, right? No matter how still you stand, no matter how good the mirror you're holding, you're still looking at a reflection of a reflection. Can it help? Yes. Do books help us see blind spots? For sure. Will they reflect completely and perfectly what the mirror of God's Word does? No.)

God's Word helps us identify the places that need attention. But God's Word is also the cleanser that helps deal with that blemish. This is the "both/and" beauty of Scripture. It doesn't just reflect what's wrong; it's the medicine to heal what's wrong.

Nothing we do can keep us from ever getting a blemish again. Remember sanctification, being made perfectly like Christ, isn't completed here. But we can stay away from people, attitudes, and situations that create the environment where blemishes pop up. When I got home from school the day of my

> Scripture doesn't just reflect what's wrong; it's the medicine to heal what's wrong.

"pimple incident," I told my Mom what happened. She said that a greasy, sugar-filled diet, or not washing my face can lead to breakouts. I didn't know my love of pizza and Oreos could affect my skin!

I certainly hadn't been taking care of my skin. Honestly, I hadn't really thought about it at all. I didn't have anyone to blame but myself.

Friends, sanctification isn't just God's part. We are also responsible to examine ourselves, to look in the mirror and apply the medicine that keeps us "clean, clear, and under control." (That's the tagline for Clean and Clear products, but it works here.)

What things might we need to keep our lives clear of? What habits or temptations do we need to keep under control? Well, your list might not look like mine, but in the name of transparency, here's an example of one thing Scripture has prescribed for me lately.

I love a good Netflix binge. I've watched *The Crown, Downton Abbey,* and *Gilmore Girls* more times than I can count. But Proverbs 23 talks a lot about appetites that we don't keep in check. I like to think this is just about food, but it's not. This particular proverb is admonishing us to be wise and disciplined with food, wealth, wisdom, compliments, and all kinds of appetites. I am currently asking the Lord how He'd like me to navigate my Netflix habits and free time.

Okay, this one I'm kind of embarrassed to admit. But I have to be super careful watching romantic movies, and I'm not talking the hot and heavy ones. I never watch those. But a good, saccharine-sweet Hallmark channel movie? Those are the ones where I have to be careful (which is a major bummer especially in December because I love their holiday movies). You see, Chad isn't super romantic. He is faithful, hard-working, and has an unbelievable servant's heart. Like for real. It's not uncommon when I'm traveling for him to do all the laundry while I'm gone. And with four boys it can often be five or six loads at a time. But flowers, gifts, and surprises? That's not his thing. And unfortunately, he married a romantic, sappy kind of girl.

When I watch those romantic kinds of movies, I can become hyper-focused on what those guys do. All the sweet, surprise gestures make my heart swoon. If I'm not careful, I'll start to wonder, "Why doesn't Chad do that?" "If he loved me that much, he'd surprise me with flowers for no reason." "Where is my horse-drawn carriage through the freshly fallen leaves?" Ridiculous!

That's kind of crazy, right? Those movies aren't real. Do we ever see the part where the romantic lead leaves his dirty clothes all over the floor? Nope. (By the way, my Chad has never done that.) Do we see their selfish ambition or vanity? (Because very few guys can look that polished and coiffed without a team of assistants and stylists.) Do we see him get up and spend time every day in the Word so he can lead his family well?

Listen, for most women those movies are probably fine. But for me, (and I'm legit, so embarrassed to admit this) I can start to wish that my husband was more like that. And friend, that's just lust. Some may downplay it and say it's "PG" lust, but for my heart, it really is lust. Here's where 1 John 2:16 calls me to obedience, "For all that is in the world—the desires of the flesh and the desires of the eyes and pride of life—is not from the Father but is from the world" (ESV). I have to bring this temptation under the lordship of Jesus, believe the best about my husband, and trust that God gave Him to me to bless and refine me.

And, it's worth saying, flowers and carriage rides aren't wrong, but in real life, nothing is more romantic than an empty laundry basket or dishwasher.

Without God's Word reflecting to me the pure and faithful love of Jesus and revealing the unlovely parts of me, I would have ignored my Hallmark blemish. And you know the worst part about these kinds of "surprise skin situations"? They pop up at the most embarrassing times. But when it comes to the ignored or hidden sins we all have, we aren't trying to protect our ego from embarrassment. No. We want to protect and promote the name and fame of Jesus.

> The first step in our part of sanctification is *confessing* the blemishes Scripture reveals.

Friends, let's be committed to checking the mirror—God's Word—daily. This is why John calls us to confess sin and pursue obedience. So there it is: when it comes to our part in sanctification, our very first pursuit is acknowledging sin in the camp, looking to Scripture to show us the blemish we've ignored. In other words, the first step in our part of sanctification is *confession*.

This is why John calls us to confess sin and pursue obedience. Confession acknowledges the sin in our camps, the blemishes on our souls, but obedience seeks to fill them not with idols or idleness, but with the Word of God. Put another way, confession sees the blemish. Obedience applies God's Word to minimize it and heal it.

If we don't apply God's Word to those blemishes in our life, if we don't let Him heal what's going on underneath, we will try to hide or cover it up. And most of us know that concealer rarely looks natural. More often than not, we end up drawing attention to the blemish we are trying to conceal. Because it's not gone, it's just (poorly) camouflaged.

As we hold up the mirror—God's Word—to see ourselves clearly and inspect for any "sin in the camp," we allow it to push us to the first step of our part in sanctification: *confessing* the blemishes that Scripture reveals. Once Scripture shows us the blemish, the second step in our part of sanctification is *obeying* it in order for the blemish to be healed.

> The second step in our part of sanctification is *obeying* Scripture in order for the blemish to be healed.

But it's often not as easy as just doing what He tells us, unfortunately. No, there are so many competing "solutions" for filling our gaps and fixing our blemishes.

Turning from Idols

When I was a resolution-maker, every January I would make personal resolutions—commitments to lose weight, pray more, and gossip less. I wanted to be faithful. I intended to stick it out. I really did. But my best intentions rarely supported long-term commitment. By February 1 (okay, by January 15), I'd usually fallen back into old patterns, my New Year commitments abandoned.

My spiritual life is much the same. A Sunday morning sermon provokes a desire to change, persevere, or grow in an area, but Monday morning habits hamper my progress. Do you know that struggle? It's that hard place where our promises don't match our perseverance, where our faith rarely matches our follow-through. Why is that?

This may not be your struggle. But it is mine, and it was Israel's. In Joshua 24 we see the people of Israel once again recommitting themselves to the Lord, also known as renewing the covenant. Joshua 24:24 records: "And the people said to Joshua, 'We will serve the LORD our God and obey him.'"

This had happened multiple times just since the Exodus. Through a chosen leader (Moses or Joshua), God called the people to reaffirm their devotion to Him.

Before we go further, let's consider the overwhelming grace of God. Our perfect, holy God allows a feeble, faithless people the opportunity to recommit themselves to Him! God not only initiates the covenant but also invites them to return to Him. He chooses to enter into a sacred agreement with Israel, and He calls them to begin again when they violate that agreement. Truly amazing!

But back to Israel. Though they had failed before, today was a new day for them. It might not have been January 1st, but they were getting an opportunity for a fresh start. If you read the whole chapter, God's call comes with a command. To walk with God, they would have to walk away from other gods. To turn toward God would mean turning away from something else. This is always true. And I think this may help me understand why I often fail to follow through on my promises. I want God, but I don't want to give up other things. I want obedience, but not necessarily sacrifice. I want to be faithful, but I also want to be comfortable. And the tension makes me sick. Friend, we can't be both comfortable and faithful.

Comfort in our current patterns was not God's invitation to Israel, nor is it to you and me. His invitation is to turn toward Him, but it is a call to turn away from idols. The idols that often receive our worship, our time, our money, our best efforts. Perhaps this is the key to turning our promises into perseverance, our faith into follow-through. We have to give up things in order to gain God. When it comes to our part in sanctification, that's the third step: not just confessing our blemishes and then obeying God's Word so that they may be healed, but actually forsaking what we were obeying before.

> The third step in our part of sanctification is *turning* from idols: forsaking what we were obeying before.

We could choose to focus on what God asks us to give up. (Because giving up those things is never easy, right?) Or we can choose to focus on what, or rather Who, we gain. It's our choice. And as it relates to our holiness and sanctification, choices are part of the pursuit.

Loving One Another

As we read John's instructions for the confident and unashamed, let's take note that he is commending these instructions to Christians. John encourages this practice of regular confession, repentance, and obedience to believers, those who have already professed faith in Christ.

So what sins might we need to bring to Him to cover and forgive us for? John says that we must grow not just in our internal sanctification, but also external love for our fellow siblings in the Lord. We must mimic the love Christ demonstrated for us, His brothers and sisters (Heb. 2:11). John wants us to believe that faithful disciples of Jesus follow His commands and love one another.

John then adds an idea we've seen before: that turning our affections *toward* one another requires us turning our affections *from* the world. As we pursue the Lord's will and as He changes our hearts, we fall more in love with Jesus and less in love with the pleasures and pursuits of this world.

I've said often that if my life involved just me and Jesus, I'd look considerably more holy than I do most of the time. Living with people is hard. Not because they are selfish and difficult (though they are sometimes) but more personally, because I am selfish and difficult.

Not long ago, Chad and I were having an argument.

Anybody else married to their polar opposite? Truly, Chad and I could not be more different. He's a type A engineer, and I'm a highly emotional, artistic thinker. He lives in the black and white; I thrive in the gray. But we are both firstborns and extremely stubborn. Not a good combination. It's sad when the only thing you have in common with your spouse is your sin natures. Mercy.

Back to our recent argument. I honestly can't remember exactly what we were arguing about, but as we were "discussing" the situation, I was running my own commentary in my mind. I remember thinking over and over, *I can't believe I married someone this selfish.* Y'all! Don't worry, you'll not be reading a book on healthy, biblical marriage from me any time soon. Maybe ever.

Now what did my patient, thoughtful, hard-working husband do to bring out this kind of passive-aggressive nastiness from his bride? He didn't do what I wanted him to do. Friend, let the irony of that wash over you. My charge? He is selfish. Why? Because he didn't do what *I* wanted him to do. It's actually kind of shocking that he hasn't left me yet. And I try to remember every day that his staying has little to do with me, and everything to do with Jesus.

What's my point besides that I'm heinously sinful? That relationships are hard. If I only had to live confident and unashamed before Jesus, well, life would be a bit easier. Now, not perfect, mind you. I'm still that same selfish girl all by myself. But she shows up quite a bit more often in my relationships.

So how do we pursue the process of sanctification—confident and unashamed—not just with God, but with others? It starts with taking the internal steps we talked about in this chapter (confession as God's Word points out our blemishes, obeying God's Word in order to heal, and turning from idols).But then it bleeds over into what we will discuss next: the ideal of transparency in our external relationships. We want to live a life that is free from duplicity and fakeness. As we confess our junk, we want to be surrounded by people who do the same. We want to be free to be ourselves and we expect others to act in kind. Do you agree? If so, let's explore that idea next.

Broken but Better

It's impossible to live before Jesus as confident and unashamed if we aren't living with others in a similar manner.

For a book about being sick of "me," we've spent a lot of time talking about self. We've spent half our time together talking about our struggle for peace, pursuing the process of holiness, and settling the question of who occupies the throne of our hearts. Why on earth camp out on all that? Because our external relationships are almost always a reflection of our internal relationship with Jesus.

Without the surrender to the process of sanctification, there's chaos in my soul. We are foolish if we think that the casualties of that kind of war are only *our* peace of heart and mind. And the fallout is usually swift, fierce, and pervasive to those around me.

A soul at war will sour relationships.

You see, maybe the worst and most devastating effect of self-help is that it looks to everyone else to fix or address what's wrong inside of me. Sanctification, on the other hand, admits that only God can fix me. And until He does, my relationships will suffer.

> A soul at war will
> sour relationships.

Self-help will make everyone else suffer for what we won't let God fix.

The degree to which we are unhappy in our relationships is likely the very same degree to which we've made those relationships about us. Let me interject that the state of a relationship falls on a wide scale that ranges from healthy to harmful. And clearly abusive relationships are an extreme that is exempt from this conversation. But within the scope of normal, non-abusive relationships, our frustrations may indicate our need for control. Often times, our disappointments can reflect our selfish expectations.

Our relationships have a tendency to become very, very much about us.

I bet a few of you, like me, have some super hard relationship situations in your life.

When I'm dealing with a hard relationship, I can convince myself that it is everybody else's problem. And you know what, I am pretty good at it. I can produce a list a mile long of what *she* did that led us here. I can point to a hundred different things that *he* said or didn't do that hurt us long before I hurt him. In my mind, I can take account of every offense and I could draw a hard line to whose fault it was and where they went wrong. Friend, let that be a warning. When we look for a reason to blame someone else, we will almost always find it. People are broken, sin-sick, and selfish.

But then again, so are we.

In the middle of one of those hard seasons of friendship, I spent a long breakfast meal with my friend Lindsey. I poured my heart out, and it was ugly and unedited. My case was pretty solid. I was methodical and merciless. I told her how wrong everyone was. I was hurting and she listened for far longer than most friends would have. When I finally came up for air, she filled the silence with this, "Whit, it's simply a reminder that people are broken and selfish. And I know this, friend, because I am. Without the daily presence of the Holy Spirit, we can't restrain our flesh. We need Him to pull those weeds and grow His spiritual fruit. We need Him desperately because we are so, so broken."

She was so, so right. Their offense wouldn't have been so great if I hadn't been so offend-able. The hurt would have felt more temporal if my perspective had been more eternal. Yes, I can't fix them, but praise Jesus, He can fix me.

So like so many other situations we've described, putting Jesus on the throne and letting Him conform us into His image doesn't often change our circumstances. People will still disappoint. Relationships will still sting and be tense. But He can change how we respond.

> Our heartaches will always feel more temporary if our hearts are anchored to eternity.

His gracious hand reaches down, cups our chins, and turns our gaze off the hurt of today and invites us to consider eternity. The Lifter of our head will always move to lessen our hurts by casting our hope on heaven.

If the hard relationship struggles have taught me anything, it's not that people can't be trusted. It's that *I* can't be trusted. I'm not in charge. I don't know how to run my life to avoid hurt, pain, discouragement, and abandonment. I can't keep myself happy because I can't keep other people happy. I can't control my own life because I can't control other people's lives. My happiness cannot rest solely on the external circumstances of my life or how others perceive or treat me. This fight for control leads to self-absorption and self-help. And again, we are naïve if we think that the wounds of war are only in our soul.

This world is broken, its inhabitants more so. But this is the address for you and me. We are broken people living in a broken place. It's our currency. We buy, sell, and exchange hurts without regard for one another, and that's not just the description for those outside of the church. No. It's shockingly true for those of us who occupy rows and pews on Sunday morning. And we are wounding each other over and over and over again.

Church folks aren't the polished, perfect people we sometimes pretend to be or that others perceive us to be. We are, as I said, broken people. But as the church, the body of Christ, we are gathered up into a community or collection of broken pieces. Think of it this way. Have you ever seen a stained-glass window? The collection of all those sharp, cracked, and imperfect pieces work together *because* of their brokenness to make something extraordinary. Any piece by itself seems useless. Alone or if not handled with care, the individual, sharp pieces can even hurt. But together they are spectacular. The sum total is more glorious than the individual pieces could ever be alone. And in the hands of a Master Craftsman, the damaged pieces have order, design, and purpose. And in that way, their brokenness becomes beautiful.

That's us: the broken, beautiful church.

If all that is true, how can our relationships be the diagnostic for our spiritual health? How do my external relationships give insight into my relationships with Jesus?

Unfortunately, community is messy. Doing life with other Christ-followers isn't a neat and tidy prospect. God has chosen to gather up a bunch of selfish, broken people together and use them to demonstrate His great love, power, and grace to a lost world. Sadly, as broken people we have a nasty habit of cutting each other.

Have you ever felt abandoned by a friend? Maybe someone has challenged the authenticity of your faith? It stings, doesn't it? When we live in community with people, they are going to misunderstand and judge us. This pain Paul knew all too well. The believers at Corinth were Paul's dear friends and fruit of a life spent proclaiming the gospel. But false prophets had infiltrated the beloved church trying to discredit Paul's apostleship and essentially the legitimacy of Christ's call on his life.

We don't know the exact source of the charge. Apparently, there was some perception that Paul was being weak in dealing with certain matters. This "weakness" made them question Paul. So Paul responds with a letter to the church at Corinth. He says in 2 Corinthians 13:5, "Examine yourselves to see whether you are in the faith; test yourselves. Do you not realize that Christ Jesus is in you—unless, of course, you fail the test?"

In response to the charge, Paul does something remarkable, and I think his example is one we could all follow when we think about how to live in the context of Christian community.

First, Paul acknowledges his weakness and points to Christ's example (2 Cor. 13:4). What a testimony of true faith! In all things, Paul points to Christ! He turns his critics to the example of Jesus who was crucified in weakness yet lives in God's power! Christ willingly laid down His life. He died a brutal and violent death though He was innocent of any crime. To many this is the picture of weaknesses, but in God's kingdom, Jesus' power was never more evident. Somehow, His brokenness in that moment on the cross was better than any other plan for our salvation. In His "weaknesses," Jesus defeated sin and death, bringing life and restoration to His followers!

God uses our weaknesses to show Himself strong. In 1 Corinthians 1:27, Paul says it this way, "But God chose the foolish things of the world to shame the wise; God chose the weak things of the world to shame the strong." Paul's "weaknesses" leave room for God to work and for God to get the glory. The same should go for us; we should see our brokenness as better—a better place to receive grace, a better posture for us to see God really move, and a better position to be sanctified.

Second, Paul takes the message of the gospel to a more personal level. He says the proof of His authority and apostleship is in the examination of the lives of the Corinthians themselves. Now Paul is not taking credit for their salvation. That is clearly a work of the Spirit; Paul would never take that glory for himself. Perhaps Paul is inviting them to look to what the Spirit has done in and among them; to look to the Spirit's wisdom in discerning their own salvation. To trust the Spirit's clarifying truth regarding Paul's apostleship. Their lives are his proof!

Second Corinthians is a letter of discipleship. Paul is teaching the believers at Corinth how to apply Jesus' teachings. Multiple times Paul has encouraged them to follow his pattern as he follows Christ. Now in his final comments, Paul says this to the charge against his authority—look at my life's work, look to your lives!

When we want to communicate the substance of our faith, perhaps we could follow Paul's example. People will know not just who we are but who Jesus is by our lives. But the sobering question for me is can I say with Paul, "Look at my life"? Perhaps this is the picture of Christian maturity when our lives speak louder than our words.

The process of sanctification has to come full circle. It's not completed on this side of eternity, but we will continue the process over and over again. Think of it like a massive filter. Each time we go around we also tighten the circle, moving closer to the center—holiness. The place where Jesus is and where we will be with Him forever. Perfectly holy. Perfectly sanctified. We are being broken daily, but with each breaking, submission and recovery happens faster. Jesus closes the gap a little bit more between where we were and where He is. We are better for the breaking. Are we perfect? No. But are we better? Well, if we are being sanctified, rather than dabbling in self-help, then the answer is yes. And that's a story worth sharing. We aren't just broken. We are better than broken.

Avoiding the Transparency Trap, Part 1: Beyond the Bad and Believing the Best

Though our lives themselves should show Christ off just by looking at them, there is a part of our Christian life that does require words. Often Christ calls us to communicate the gospel in ways that are more than just actions. Remember that one of the definitions of *confidence* is to speak with clarity and boldness. What we say about our lives and the gospel of Jesus looks different if we are talking with people outside the faith, and those who are inside our church bubble.

If we are honest with ourselves, most of us would admit that we live inside a pretty legit church bubble. What I mean is that most people we engage with are a lot like us—also living inside the church bubble, unless we have those "one-off" encounters," as I call them. You know, where you strike up a conversation with your hairstylist about something more serious than the weather or how her kids are doing in school. Or perhaps we chat it up with the gal pumping gas next to us at the gas station. Then there are the polite, but kind of awkward, random conversations with the lady behind you, loading her items onto the conveyor as you finish checking out at the grocery store. Those are not the norm for me.

Sick of Me

Because we are so insulated, we kind of share this "language" in the church.

One of the things that has become really interesting are these "buzz" words that now are pervasive in the church bubble, inside Christian culture—things like "community," "fellowship," "transparency," "honesty," "getting real," and "authenticity." There is a prevailing argument that younger generations are disenfranchised with what has been traditionally called "church" or "religion." The older generation has been called "plastic," "pretend," or "perfect." These opposing ideas seem to define the options for spiritual community (in some circles even the word *church* is a bit too polarizing or antiquated)—either be totally transparent, holding all your sinful junk up like a banner to celebrate under, or totally fake, with everything swept under the rug.

Every single time I go somewhere and teach, the one comment I always get is, "I love how transparent you are." I don't keep much of anything hidden. And it is a goal of mine to share all the things and not to gloss over it to make myself appear more or better than I am. But I've heard this so often, I started to ask myself what it means. What do they mean when they say they love how "transparent" I am? I mean, I think I know. I think what they are saying is that they believe that the person on the stage is the same gal you'd bump into at Wal-Mart, except that I'd have on less makeup, a ball cap, and maybe not a bra. (If we're being really honest.)

I'm super grateful that anyone would enjoy anything about my teaching. But I began to wonder, *What is the spiritual value to this "transparency"? What spiritual need is being met? Not just for them but for me? Why do they value this kind of honesty? And*

126

why do I offer it? But there was a deeper question: Is this valuable for the kingdom?

Does this virtue that seems to be so super important in the church bubble have gospel value?

What people want in a church and in relationships are transparency and community. But what is the biblical grounding for that? To find the answer, I began to research these ideals to try and find their place in Scripture. If we are going to value a virtue above all others in relationships and the church, it ought to be a biblical virtue, right? And please forgive me if this is selfish, but I thought, *If I'm going to be known for something, for anything, I sure hope it's something that has real, eternal benefit.* And I hoped, really prayed, I'd find some sweet proverb that extolled the praise of the transparent woman. (Spoiler alert: it's not a part of the Proverbs 31 woman description.) In fact, transparency and community aren't really anywhere in Scripture. At least not in the ways we define them.

At best these are secondary virtues. They certainly aren't headliners. They aren't front and center. To be in a place where people "get me," where I "get them" and where we are in community with one another is really hard to define and ground in Scripture. I'm not saying that it's not a good pursuit. But it's not a *primary* pursuit. And "transparency"? It's only mentioned one place, *one place*, in all of Scripture. In Revelation 21:21, we have a description of the street of gold of the new Jerusalem. It's the place where God's people will live with Him for all eternity. There the streets are made of pure gold, "as pure as transparent glass."

That's it. That's all we get regarding "transparent." We are going to look a little bit later at places where the idea of honesty and sincerity are briefly explained. But just for minute, consider how unusual it is that one of the most valued, talked about, and desired aspects of spiritual life is not equally valued in Scripture.

It makes me wonder, why is this so important to me, and to you?

Transparency. Community. Honesty. Sincerity. Brokenness. Fellowship. These are all virtues, I think. Good things that ought to define biblical relationships. It is good and holy for us to say, "I love Jesus, but I am broken. Here are my failures as a believer. I want you to know the truth about me."

But what if, what if these are fruits of a pursuit, not a pursuit in and of themselves? It's interesting and sobering that these virtues get so much air time in conversations, but not much ink time in Scripture.

So when we say we want "community" or "transparency," what do we really mean? I'm happy to admit that the idea is more than just the word. And perhaps the idea is in Scripture. But in order to find out, we need to know exactly what we mean when we want these things. It reminds me of the line in *The Princess Bride*. Vizzini keeps saying incredulously, "Inconceivable!" Inigo looks at him at the edge of the Cliffs of Insanity and says, "You keep using that word. I do not think it means what you think it means."

When we say "transparency" and "community," I just have to say, "I do not think it means what you think it means."

When we say that we desire transparency, I think what we think we are saying is that we desire to know who another person authentically is.

When I go into my boys' classroom for the first time each school year and I survey all the moms dropping off their kids, I'm looking for the moms who are like me.

Are her kid's supplies labeled with his name on each item? Yes. Oh and good gravy, with a printed out label? She's way out of my league.

Oh, she signed up for Room Mom. Yeah, we probably couldn't be friends. I'm the mom who has to be harassed to turn in the permission slip. I would drive her bananas.

Look, she came in workout clothes, and her body fits the uniform. I bet her spandex has actually seen the inside of a gym. No doubt she'd think I'm a fraud. Who am I kidding? I am a fraud.

Maybe you have a similar dialogue when you walk into church or Bible study. Women are brilliant at sizing up the room to see where we fit in.

Oh she's the "legit" Bible study girl. Look, her workbook already looks broken in. The corners are crunched and dog-eared. I bet all her answers are complete. No blanks for her. I'll be a complete disappointment.

Look at her Bible; well, I mean first she actually remembered to bring it. I'm going to "just use my phone" like it's an intentional life choice. Her Bible is actually worn. I'm sure she knows exactly where Malachi is. Nope, not sitting by her.

Aw man, she put on makeup, actual makeup for today. Why didn't somebody tell me it was that kind of event? Goodness gracious I'm still wearing yesterday's mascara. Next, please!

Great, she brought the snack. I'm the loser who just showed up. Oh mercy, there's not one soul here like me!

We do this all the time in a thousand ways and scenarios. And for those of us alive and breathing millennial air (whether you were born in that actual generation or not), we are constantly surveying the real *and* digital world around us wondering, *Who is like me?*

Maybe this is the plight of twenty-first-century women. Maybe it is the current we have to swim against. We are so used to seeing the picture of perfect, that we're desperate to know someone "real." Someone who isn't "perfect." Because you and I know our own realities. We are far from perfect.

But wait a minute, if I'm not perfect, perhaps Miss Sweats-in-Her-Spandex and Miss Worn-in-Workbook isn't perfect either. Here's the life altering, shame-shifting, community-building truth. She isn't perfect. And she doesn't want you to be.

How on earth could I possibly know this? Because I'm not perfect, and I don't expect you to be. If we were bold enough to live transparency without simply pleading for it, we'd discover the truth. What if we walked into a room of women and said, "Hey girls, I went to bed wearing my mascara and put on workout clothes from yesterday because they were on the floor next to my bed. Oh, and when I say 'workout clothes,' I use that term very, very loosely (even if my yoga pants aren't). Will you still be my friend?" Most women would say, "ABSOLUTELY!"

And that woman who seems to be totally put together? She might have on super cute flats from Target or even Nordstrom, and maybe her makeup is Instagram-worthy but I'd bet you she has her own list of insecurities. She would probably look at us and think, *If only I could be as confident and relaxed as her. Not so consumed with what everybody is thinking.*

Really. Every woman in every room is wishing there is something about her that could go unnoticed or stay hidden. Some of us overcompensate to try and distract from our "obvious" flaws. We're the girl talking about the dollar section at Target, so you won't ask me about my unhappy marriage. We're the girl drinking water, so I appear healthy even though I am ashamed that I failed to "meal plan" and had to feed my kids Chick-fil-A . . . again. We're the girl who makes sure my earrings match my perfect outfit so that you'll be kind of impressed with me when I can't answer that really hard question on page 13 of the Bible study we're doing.

Some of us hide completely, never letting anything or anyone draw attention to us at all.

Maybe that's Pollyanna of me. Maybe you've been on the not-so-generous side of the circle. Maybe you've been the outsider that clearly wasn't welcome. Oh friend, I'm sorry. I'm so, so sorry. I know those experiences are real. I know they exist. I know what it's like to be unwelcome and clearly on the outside. I know what it's like to be ridiculed and shamed. (Remember the cheerleader story?)

Not long ago I posted a story on my Facebook page that ignited a bit of a mommy war on my page. Here's the post:

> So after today, I'll have rising 6th, 4th, and 2nd graders. (Not pictured, my future Pre-Ker.) It's their last day of school, and I'm missing awards day. Just in case I over-glamorize this ministry life, this is it. You miss stuff. You feel guilty. You stay in your lane. You shake it off and go serve the kingdom. My call is no greater than any other mama's. Just different.
>
> People ask often how I do it all. Here's the answer. I don't. I miss awards day. I forget the

teacher's birthday. I don't do Pinterest parties; we do Chuck E. Cheese. I'm not Room Mom. I can't go on all the field trips.

I tell people all the time that I struggle. Big time. I love my people so much it hurts. But I've prayed, interceded, and agonized. This is my conclusion. God loves them more than I do. I don't think He's going to punish them because I'm obeying His call. In 15 or 20 years I'm praying Chad Capps and I have boys who know they aren't the center of our world. I'm not sure that's a bad lesson. Yes, Jesus, be the center. Today. Tomorrow. Always.

Mamas who go to everything, remember everything, home-make everything, your selfless sacrifice teaches that lesson too! We say it with our lives. But here's what I'm learning, our inability to do-it-all, bring-it-all, be-it-all, leaves wonderful voids for Jesus to fill.

Today Jesus is filling that gap by an amazing husband and dad who leaves his ridiculously high-pressure job to attend four awards ceremonies. He prays me up and cheers them on!! He texts me mid-ceremony. And I think, "I'm so glad I'm not there."

Mamas, don't sweat the cracks in your lane. Jesus fills them just fine.

Sometimes I forget that social media is less social, more media. You know, the investigative, get-the-dirt, confrontational kind? Some women said I was taking my kids for granted and asking God to cover up my selfishness and poor choices. Ouch. Apparently to some gals, it sounded like I was bragging on my husband, and that was offensive. One woman commented something to the effect, "Some of us don't have husbands or help." (While her comment and others like it weren't the majority, there were enough to make it clear I struck a nerve.)

I was so bummed. The genuine point of the post was to help mamas who, like me, suffer from the guilt of not being able to do it all. I hated that I'd made that woman feel worse about her life. But then I thought about it honestly. The truth is, I was bragging on my husband. He's so selfless. He supports me without question. And I don't get credit for that. That's Chad. All Chad. And while I wanted to encourage all the other mamas, I also wanted to honor him. Because the truth is, he deserved it.

You see, there is an interesting contradiction buried in our desire for transparency. We want to see what's broken and dysfunctional. But if something is good, lovely, or pure, we don't really want that kind of transparency.

Honestly, I get it. Goodness gracious, I've done exactly what this friend did to me. I've looked at posts and pictures and thought, *Must be nice.* Rather than being happy for her, her happiness makes me sad. That's just straight crazy!

Yes, every woman is jacked up in her own specific way. I know this. You know this, right? I haven't stumbled across something profound. I didn't write this book to convince you and me that everyone around us is broken. If there is a benefit to living in this generation, it's that most of us have come to the realization that what we see isn't likely what we get. A filter here, a cropped image there, and things appear much better than they really are. What's posted isn't all there is.

Believing the Best

No doubt we are tired of the filtered and fake. But let's be gracious and generous. It would be good for us to practice a little positivity and give people the benefit of the doubt. In the absence of proof, let's believe the best about her. Because believing the worst can actually be the worst.

There's this dude in the Old Testament named Hanun, and not believing the best about David cost him dearly.

In 2 Samuel 10:2–3 we read, "David thought, 'I will show kindness to Hanun son of Nahash, just as his father showed kindness to me.' So David sent a delegation to express his sympathy to Hanun concerning his father. When David's men came to the land of the Ammonites, the Ammonite commanders said to Hanun their lord, 'Do you think David is honoring your father by sending envoys to you to express sympathy? Hasn't David sent them to you only to explore the city and spy it out and overthrow it?'"

During my first job, I was encouraged to read Norman Vincent Peale's *The Power of Positive Thinking*. I remember thinking that I liked the idea but feeling that positivity couldn't possibly dramatically alter the course of my life. Life is messy and hard, and the negativity can't always be negated with positivity.

Years later, I don't think my opinion has changed as it relates to life's situations. But I do think that positivity has a powerful place in our relationships. In 2 Samuel 10, David learns of the death of a political ally. David decides to send a delegation of men to show his respect and sorrow over the death of the Ammonite king.

Hanun, the former king's son, has succeeded his father on the throne. He listens to the speculation of his leaders and chooses to believe that David's intentions are malicious. David must have sent these men here to spy on the city, they conclude.

Hanun responds by seizing, assaulting, and humiliating David's men. To forcibly remove a Jewish man's beard made him an outcast and a violator of Levitical law (Lev. 19:27). Further, to desecrate their robes and reveal their genitals publicly was horribly denigrating. David shows tender care for his men when, in response, he tells them to stay in Jericho until their beards have been regrown. Jericho is the first city they would have passed through after returning from the Ammonite country. This would spare them further humiliation by returning home in shame to their families and royal court.

David's response to Hanun and the Ammonite people is less gracious. The rest of the chapter records David's shrewd military mind and successful conquest of the Ammonites and their allies.

All this carnage because Hanun chose to believe the worst about David, rather than the best. If Hanun had used a little positivity, or simply chosen to take David at his word, Hanun could have maintained peace in the land and for his people.

When we look for the worst in people, we will usually find it. Evidenced in 2 Samuel 9 and David's care for Mephibosheth, David was gracious and merciful, even to the family of the man who hunted and tried to kill him. David's integrity would have kept peace with Hanun because of the treaty David had with Nahash, Hanun's father.

I'm not suggesting that everyone deserves this kind of Pollyanna positivity; we should not ever turn a blind eye to hurt or abuse. We should be as Jesus commanded, "as shrewd as snakes and as innocent as doves" (Matt. 10:16). But when someone's motives seem unclear, we may avoid unnecessary conflict if we first choose to believe the best before assuming the worst.

Let's pretend for just a minute that even part of what we see about someone else's life is legit. What if her house is that picture perfect without cropping and editing? What if her kids really are that awesome and kind? Because what if the girl who brought her Bible study book all filled in, whose Bible is all highlighted and marked up really does, I mean *really does*, just pour her heart and mind into loving Jesus?

What if the mom who remembered the snacks did it because it's her joy to serve others through hospitality? What if that girl who seems all pulled together enjoys (in the holiest way) the creativity of fashion and expressing it in her own attire? Is there really anything wrong with the woman who is faithful day in and day out to take care of her body? What if she just truly believes that her body is a temple to the Lord and He deserves her attention and discipline?

It's not all real for sure, but it may not be completely fake either. Why would I judge her and assume it's not? Is it because it makes me feel better to believe it's fake? Why do we often assume that if a woman is better than us in some way, she's inauthentic? Can we get gut honest for a minute? That reaction says way more about me than it says about her.

Can I speak something over us, our generation? I don't mean Boomers, Xers, Xennials, or Millennials. I mean those of us alive right now, living in this moment and trying to define biblically what it means to be feminine *and* a follower of Christ. What if we let one another be truly transparent? What if that transparency meant we could celebrate the good Jesus is doing in our life *and* the areas where we are struggling. Transparency can't be just airing all the bad.

What if we let her successes not make us feel like failures? Can you imagine how different our churches might look if we celebrated one another's victories, gave voice to the Jesus-growth happening in our hearts and homes, and cheered one another on to holiness?

What if we didn't expect one another to be perfect, but we didn't demand that each of us be completely jacked up either? What if you could freely talk about the areas where you are growing in Christlikeness and at the same time ask for help in the areas where you struggle? What if *that* was what we considered real transparency? Can you even imagine?

> Transparency can't be just airing all the bad.

Beyond Brokenness

I think one of the greatest wins for the devil over the last fifteen to twenty years has been to convince us that if we give God credit for what He's done in us, people (specifically women) will think we are bragging. Brokenness has become the devil's weapon of choice. It's cool to gather and commiserate around the sin and celebrate how much we all wallow in it without a real desire to move *out* of the sin into change. It's cool to stay in the trench; if we don't, we are fake or inauthentic. Seems backwards, right? Oh, but that's why it's been so, so effective.

Satan's plan goes something like this. (Don't be surprised to hear him use spiritual ideas. He is brilliant at twisting them. It was his first tactic in the garden. He's had the same trick on repeat ever since.)

"Jesus wants you to go into all the world and make disciples, right? Well, to make disciples you really need to be in a relationship with people first, right? You know that people these days don't want to feel all judged. They will only respond to someone who is real and broken. This culture doesn't want easy, simple Sunday school answers. They want to see the mess of your life. Don't whitewash it. Be raw and vulnerable. Otherwise you'll appear hypocritical. And there's no way you can be effective if you're a hypocrite, right? If you get all holy on them, you'll lose them."

Now before I go any further, let me acknowledge, there's some truth in that. But where the devil is concerned, a half-truth is a whole lie. We do need to care about people. We ought to be authentic. We should avoid being hypocritical at all costs. (More on that in a bit.)

But look at the lie the devil is selling. *Don't let the gospel do its work. Don't show them that this thing really works. Don't live like Jesus can actually change your life for the better. And for sure don't give evidence or testimony to the fact!*

Further handicapping the church, we don't disciple because we've bought the brokenness thing—hook, "lie," and sinker. We can't disciple one another if we're all so completely broken. So only a few churches in America focus on women helping women grow closer to Jesus. Why? Because we're so afraid we will be judged, and not just by the lost, but by believers! Oh friends, we have stripped the gospel of all its power when we don't give God glory for making us more than broken. Like we touched on in the last chapter, He is making us *better* than broken!

It makes me weep that we've let him win this battle. Oh, sweet friend, I want to grab you and me both by the shoulders and shake us awake. We have to stop putting asterisks (*) by the gospel. We have to stop pretending that it isn't life-altering power and hope. But what's the proof of that? I am. And friend, you are too. It's time we live confident and unashamed that what Jesus died to give me and you is worth living and proclaiming. He *can* sanctify us and *promises* He will.

So instead of rolling up to Bible study wondering what's wrong with all these other women, what if we walked in asking ourselves what's right with her? What if we asked Jesus to do for me what He's done for her? When that happens, we avoid the transparency trap of only wanting to see the dirt, and we are freed to celebrate the beauty of Christ at work. We let the gospel be effective, not just for salvation but for sanctification as well.

There is the transparency trap where we expect people to only be authentically broken, where we refuse to believe the best about *her*. But what about the transparency traps that we fall into *ourselves*? We may extend grace to her rather than judgment, but can we do the same for ourselves? How do we live transparently before and with others?

Transparency is one of those squishy virtues that we kind of get in our culture but can't totally define. It's kind of defined by the people that value it. When I took an informal poll, friends said they think of it as being real, genuine, and authentic.

Let's first deal with authenticity. A quick search of the word *authentic* or *authenticity* doesn't give us much. When I looked through some of my favorite commentaries, any discussion of authenticity involves the trustworthiness of a particular text or book of the Bible. For example, early church fathers and scholars discussed the authenticity of Peter's writings or the Gospel of Mark.

Authenticity was something that described whether or not a source could be considered reliable. I think this tells us something about the nature of authenticity within the context of our friends and our family, but also within the greater context of those with whom we want to be witnesses for Jesus or those with whom we share the gospel. We should rightly consider our authenticity. They certainly will. Are we reliable sources? Can we be trusted? Does our message seem sincere and give evidence to who Jesus is and what He's done in our lives?

Now just because the word *authentic* doesn't appear in Scripture doesn't mean the concept isn't there. In 2 Corinthians 6, Paul admonishes those who are suffering or enduring hardship not to be a stumbling block to those around them. In this passage Paul praises the virtues of truthfulness and genuineness. I should confess I had to look that one up. Did you know it's an actual word, not an alcoholic beverage? *Genuineness* means "not counterfeit, possessing the claimed or attributed character, quality or origin, authentic; real."

This is what Paul says of his own ministry. He was genuine, sincere, and truthful. Here's the passage:

> We put no stumbling block in anyone's path,
> so that our ministry will not be discredited.

Rather, as servants of God we commend ourselves in every way: in great endurance; in
troubles, hardships and distresses; in beatings,
imprisonments and riots; in hard work, sleepless nights and hunger; in purity, understanding, patience and kindness; in the Holy Spirit
and in sincere love; in truthful speech and in the
power of God; with weapons of righteousness in
the right hand and in the left; through glory and
dishonor, bad report and good report; genuine,
yet regarded as impostors; known, yet regarded
as unknown; dying, and yet we live on; beaten,
and yet not killed; sorrowful, yet always rejoic-
ing; poor, yet making many rich; having nothing, and yet possessing everything. We have
spoken freely to you, Corinthians, and opened
wide our hearts to you. We are not withholding
our affection from you, but you are withholding
yours from us. As a fair exchange—I speak as
to my children—open wide your hearts also.
(2 Cor. 6:3–13)

We are called to be genuine, truthful, and sincere. Paul says
that servants of God commend themselves to others by acting
in a way that is consistent with the message we proclaim—the
life and ministry of Jesus. What does it mean to commend ourselves? The word means that we would present ourselves as
worthy of confidence.

(So authenticity seems to be an important virtue for the
woman who is confident and unashamed.)

Sick of Me

Does that idea make you super uncomfortable? Is it just me? When God called me to begin speaking, I was nearly immobilized by the fear that people would think I had it all together, that I had this Christianity thing all figured out. And maybe worse, what if they believed that *I thought* I was the from-the-stage subject matter expert on what it means to follow Christ?

Truly, that thought would keep me up at night. Goodness, y'all. I don't want anyone to be impressed with me. That makes my neck all splotchy and turns my stomach in knots. I absolutely don't want you to have confidence in me. So to compensate I'd highlight all my marriage mishaps and mom mistakes. There was never a shortage of material there! And you know what? It worked! I think most people who know me or those that have heard me speak would tell you that I am shockingly average. And not the least bit impressive.

And for a while, I was okay with that. Relieved actually. But over time something in my heart began to change. I felt the sting of conviction every time someone greeted me or sent me a comment along the lines of, "thank you so much for being so real." I tried to tell myself that they were just impressed with my brokenness, my transparency. But what was really happening was that they were impressed with me.

Y'all, it puts a lump in my throat to admit that. Years of trying to be unimpressive had somehow still made me the center of attention. The desire to not be on a pedestal had hijacked my pride and my focus. In all my "realness," *I was still thinking far too much about me.*

Now maybe you don't speak from a stage, but we all have a platform, a position of influence. Maybe it's to the other moms who serve on the PTA with you. Perhaps you influence your

142

partners for that group project for class. Some of us lead teams at church or work. Friends, we all have the opportunity to make a difference, even if we aren't leading. Those of us who sit shoulder to shoulder in small group or Sunday school, hang with our youth group, or do life together in singles ministry all want to point others to Jesus. To that end, we can't get overly concerned with what people think of us. We have a responsibility to be a credible witness for Christ, yes. But overemphasizing our sin can have an unintended consequence: we diminish the cross.

Brokenness isn't the only way to be a witness for Jesus. What if we can make the most influence by being better? Rather than trying to deflect glory from ourselves, what if we focused on reflecting glory back onto Him? You see, all those years I spent trying not to let people be impressed with

> Overemphasizing our sin can have an unintended consequence: we diminish the cross.

me made me miss opportunities for them to be impressed with Him. What the Lord has done in me is truly remarkable. It's uncomfortable because it calls attention to me, but the truth is, if you know me, really know me, you know it's all Him.

It's a tension to be managed for sure, and a tension that Paul talked about often. What Paul is describing here is not self-commendation for the glory of self; it's all for the glory of God. Compare what Paul says in 2 Corinthians 6 with what he says here in 2 Corinthians 4:1–3:

Therefore, since through God's mercy we have this ministry, we do not lose heart. Rather, we have renounced secret and shameful ways; we do not use deception, nor do we distort the word of God. On the contrary, by setting forth the truth plainly we commend ourselves to everyone's conscience in the sight of God. And even if our gospel is veiled, it is veiled to those who are perishing.

Why does this theme of commendation come up so often here in 2 Corinthians? Well, Paul's apostolic authority has been challenged. What he's reminding his readers and his detractors alike is that he has never polluted the Word of God or manipulated truth for his own glory or reputation. Look what he says specifically. He doesn't use deception or distort the Word of God. Instead, he states the truth of God plainly because what is proclaimed is not for Paul but for the sake of Christ Jesus.

If you read the collection of the Pauline works, you'll notice Paul never hid his flaws. He didn't whitewash, minimize, or deflate them. But neither did he shy away from giving God the glory for the work Christ had done in his life. He spoke the truth plainly. He was honest about both the weaknesses and the wins. And yet, Paul still had his critics. How could this man who said he wanted to be all things to all people for the sake of the gospel make peace with not being understood, even maligned?

I think the truth is here in both of these 2 Corinthian passages. In the 2 Corinthians 4 passage Paul explains that some truth is simply hidden from the minds of those who can't see it.

He takes neither the credit nor the blame for how people receive the truth of Jesus Christ.

Can we talk about that for just a minute? I think this is a critical issue for us to settle in our hearts. I love Paul's ability to leave all the responsibility right where it belongs, with the Lord God Himself. Oh friend, that you and I could do the same. We would never think of taking the credit for what God might do through us in the lives of others, right? But every time we own the blame for what someone may or may not think of us and Jesus, we commit a similar sin. We make too much of ourselves.

Now I can tell you I've often felt conviction for disobedience or pride regarding how I represented Christ. But here's a key distinction. Conviction comes from the Holy Spirit. Condemnation comes from self. And most of what trips us up, hijacks our confidence, or handicaps our effectiveness comes from being too "us" focused. It's my voice, not the voice of the Holy Spirit.

And friend, if there's hypocrisy in us, it is that. That the people of God would keep from pointing others to God because we are too preoccupied with ourselves. I prefer to dress it up like humility, but make no mistake, it's hypocrisy.

And here's what is so valuable for us today. If you are engaged in social media, actively reading the news, or engaging in coffee shop or water cooler discussions, you know that Christians don't have much street cred in the marketplace of ideas anymore. In fact, it's possible that we don't even start with a neutral reputation. To many, Christianity has a negative start value. We don't just lack credibility, we are saddled with the stench of hypocrisy. We have an uphill battle in gaining ground in the area of public opinion. The good news is that Paul explains how we reclaim some of the ground we may have lost.

145

Because Christians have been called hypocritical for so long, I think we've worked a little too hard to break that stereotype. We let the pendulum swing too far. We wanted to gain ground by being broken and honest in our weaknesses, but we surrendered the ground of His glory and ability to really work in our lives. In all our transparency over our sin, we forgot to tell the story of the God who can actually transform us and take us beyond brokenness. So what do we do to reverse that trend?

Paul has something to say about that.

Honest about Our Hope

One of the reasons Paul was so influential in shaping the everyday living of the life of Christ is because he didn't just tell us what to do, he told us how to do it.

According to 2 Corinthians 6, the evidence that we can be trusted is in how we live specifically in hardship and distress. What did that look like for Paul and Timothy, his companion? They endured beatings, imprisonments, riots, sleepless nights, and hunger. Those aren't foreign experiences for believers today, but they aren't typical for most of us. Perhaps to us Paul would say we ought to show endurance in marital conflict, dealing with rebellious teenagers, spiteful coworkers, difficult family members, agonizing financial difficulties, or debilitating or chronic sickness.

In any and every situation, the call is for us to show *and* tell that Jesus is truly worth it all. In the face of these and a thousand other hard circumstances, we are to be patient, kind, and sincere. Then Paul says we should be "truthful in speech and in the power of God."

Oh friend, what if *this* was our working definition of transparency? What if this kind of testimony was the one that filled our social media posts, our blogosphere, coffee shop chats, small groups, and Bible studies? What if we were honest about our struggles and sin, but hopeful and committed to the hope of sanctification? We are really good at the former, not so good at the latter. The power of God is not only promised but powerful to help us overcome hardship and sin.

What might people in and outside the church think about God if we were a people who were not just honest, but hopeful? Oh, but friend, this isn't a vapid, Pollyanna kind of hope. This hope is informed and weaponized. We aren't meant to just wish for it; we are meant to fight for it.

Paul outlines the external circumstances of the world that can be overcome with internal virtues of faith. Against battles and beatings, sleepless nights and hunger, we bring purity and patience, understanding and kindness. All of these virtues though aren't served up with a heavy dose of self-help and bootstrapping. No, all of these are done in the power of the Holy Spirit and with sincere love. This is the call of genuineness, transparency. And transparency only comes through sanctification.

Think about the last time you talked with someone about a topic that required honesty and transparency, something that required courage to share. Maybe it was a relational kind of convo, a smoothing out of a hard place or clarifying a misunderstanding. Perhaps someone asked you, "How are you?" And for a minute you were tempted to answer honestly. In all those conversations, what was your primary thought or motivation? Was it, *How can I show who I am so that they can see Christ in me?* Or did you think, *How can I answer this right or prove my point?*

The first response only happens when we are listening to the Holy Spirit and being led by love. That was Paul's encouragement. This is the overcoming stuff, the stuff that makes us look less like ourselves and more like Jesus. But the overcoming, well, that's just for us. We conquer our consuming fascination with self and trust our motives and the outcome to the Lord. Paul doesn't promise a magic pill here.

This is the Pauline theology I'd like to mark my life. Instead, I live out a misapplied thorn theology. Paul often talked about the thorn in his flesh, the thing that kept him humble (2 Cor. 12:7–10). I've often used this excerpted passage to somehow justify a "this is just the way I am" kind of fatalism. Paul's thorn was used by God for Paul's humility, not his complacency. The same goes for us.

Complacency misses the point of sanctification and the supreme power of Christ in us. We will not be perfect this side of heaven, but I don't believe that means that we are meant to forever struggle with every sin to the same degree we do today. No, according to 2 Corinthians 6, we can share our struggles and still proclaim the power of God to help us overcome those struggles. We are works of progressive holiness. We have to be as honest about that hope as we are about our sin: God *can* transform us.

> Our thorns are used by God for our humility, not our complacency.

We are held in the tension of now and not yet. We have been made right with Christ. Legally we are holy, but we are still called to pursue holiness. Is that confusing to anybody else? As we've seen before, this is the difference between justification and sanc-tification. Justification is the act of God making us legally right with Him because of our faith in Jesus Christ. Sanctification is the process of becoming more and more like Christ until we see Him face-to-face.

Why does this distinction matter? Because if we don't see the need for the ongoing work of the Holy Spirit to make us more like Christ, we remain spiritual infants. Justification imputes Christ's righteousness to us, but it does not impute His discipline and self-denial on us. This is the part of the call where we "take up our cross daily" and follow Him. Sanctification is a both/and partnership between us and the Holy Spirit.

Of the many ways we can avoid the transparency trap and jump onboard the Holy Spirit's ongoing work in our hearts, I think one way is absolutely essential: understanding exactly which type of transparency we are participating in. We'll explore this in the next chapter.

Avoiding the Transparency Trap, Part 2: The Categories of Transparency

In studying transparency, I've discovered that it's kind of transactional. There is the way in which others present themselves to us and the way in which we present ourselves to others. There is a give and take, and the giving and the taking isn't always equal. We don't always get what we expect, and we don't always give what others deserve. But regardless of what side of the equation we are on, transparency usually originates from a few specific motivations. Let's look at transparency in three distinct categories—immature transparency, premature transparency, and mature transparency. I've been guilty of all three, and I've witnessed all three varieties.

Let's begin with *immature transparency*. Immature transparency happens when we confess something as a backhanded way of deflecting accountability or looking for illegitimate affirmation. It goes something like this: we confess a sin or weakness and then kind of write it off as not that big a deal. Or maybe it's just something that we are constantly struggling with. What's missing in the confession is any sense of brokenness. This kind of transparency often fills airtime and is used to make people think we are committed Christians when we are really more of a comfortable Christian. We do it out of a motive of wanting another person to *think* we're serious about sin, when in fact we're serious about how we look in front of that person.

We can also use this type of transparency as a kind of diversion. If I call your attention to one particular area of sin or struggle, then you won't look really hard at my life to what is actually keeping me from growing in Christlikeness. And if I beat you to the punch and "confess" it, then perhaps you won't look too hard for yourself.

In either case, we haven't yet arrived at the gospel prerequisite for transparency—brokenness. Immature transparency stinks of self-help. The goal of immature transparency is self-preservation not sanctification. We aren't sorry for the sin that keeps us stuck, and we certainly don't really intend to do anything about it. The trap of immature transparency is that we tend to glamorize or make light of sin. We can't make progress stuck in this trap.

That leads us to the second kind of transparency: *premature transparency.* Premature transparency demonstrates the brokenness and sorrow of conviction. I'd argue this is where most of us live. We hate the sins that we keep confessing over and over again. We grieve what it cost Jesus. We want to be better, do more, and change. But premature transparency doesn't invite the kind of accountability and action that achieves life change. This is where I was at the beginning of our book. My friend Krista nailed me. I had slipped into the transparency trap of believing that confessing sin is the same thing as turning from it. Let's be honest. Confession is easy. Change is hard. The trap of premature transparency is riding the emotional high of confession but never arriving at transformation.

For both immature and premature transparency, there is something else going on under the surface, and y'all, it ain't pretty. If we are completely transparent, we'd have to admit that we want her to admit her junk so that I'll feel better about mine. There's a sense that if I know you are struggling, stuck, and ineffective that I'll either feel better about my own failures or feel like at least I'm more successful than you.

There I said it. It's ugly. But it's true.

Confession shouldn't ever be used as weapon to keep others at arm's length or a prop to make us feel better about ourselves. If confession is abused we've fallen into the trap of transparency and missed the point of transformation.

Have you ever sat in church, heard a sermon, and thought, *That's not me. I don't do that.* Or tried to defend your behavior by thinking, *Well, at least I'm not as bad as so-and-so.* I've had both those slippery thoughts, and they can quickly lead to the dangerous place of self-justification. And we will often use transparency as the springboard for this kind of self-help.

That's what is meant by the word *sneer* in Luke 16:14–15:

> The Pharisees, who loved money, heard all this and were sneering at Jesus. He said to them, "You are the ones who justify yourselves in the eyes of others, but God knows your hearts. What people value highly is detestable in God's sight."

The Pharisees sneered at Jesus after He told a parable to illustrate the corrupting power of money and influence. Jesus closes the parable saying, "No one can serve two masters. Either you will hate the one and love the other, or you will be devoted to the one and despise the other. You cannot serve both God and money" (Luke 16:13).

Not only do the Pharisees sneer at Jesus, but they disregard or mock His lordship. It's rarely good to be in the same camp as the Pharisees, and sadly, I've been in that camp before. Unfortunately, this passage revealed my Pharisee-heart.

These Pharisees wanted to justify themselves in order to appear righteous or holy. This was their real idol. Money was a symptom, but the real sickness was the idolatry of appearance or pride. They cared about appearing righteous more than actually being righteous. This is idolatry.

Jesus says it this way, "What people value highly is detestable in God's sight" (Luke 16:15b). This phrase *value highly* means to exalt and esteem. Money isn't detestable to God. Being consumed by money, what it affords, and how it makes us appear to others is detestable. Money is a sacrifice we make on the altar of self.

Money, like so many other passions, can become an idol. God detests idolatry. God detests pride. God hates it when we prop up our holiness on the failures of others. When we turn our noses up at truth and think, *Not me.*

Truth always has the power to transform us. How do we respond to hard truth in Scripture? Do we sneer like the Pharisees? Turn our nose up and think of a dozen other people and things worse than we are? Do we try to justify our behavior so we don't seem all that bad? Do we mock the lordship of Jesus and His authority to put His finger on sin in our lives? This is a hard truth from a hard passage. I'm far too much like the Pharisees. That's a truth that needs to transform me.

To move past immature transparency or premature transparency, we desperately need what the Pharisees were lacking—brokenness and accountability. We need a commitment to add our pursuit of His Word and His ways to His process of sanctification. But what does that look like? Well, sometimes to get a breakthrough, God has to break you.

We don't like to think that way, do we? Like me, do you think of breakthroughs as the victorious moment when your circumstances changed, a conflict was resolved, or God fixed "that person"? Yeah, those are the kinds of breakthroughs I like.

Let me say it again, to get to your breakthrough, sometimes God has to break you.

Consider Acts 10:15: "The voice spoke to him a second time, 'Do not call anything impure that God has made clean.'"

> Sometimes to get a breakthrough, God has to break you.

Two major characters are involved in this breakthrough, but it will impact the future of the entire family of God forever. That's not hyperbole. Acts 10 and its ripple effects change the face of the church. This is such a huge breakthrough.

First, we meet Cornelius, an important man in the Italian army, overseeing the region of Caesarea for Rome. Essential to this part of the story is the fact that Cornelius is a Gentile, a non-Jew by birth.

God speaks to Cornelius in a dream and tells him to send men of his household to Joppa to find Peter the apostle and ask him to come stay in Cornelius's home.

Peter's reply would likely be "no." It was forbidden for Jews to associate with Gentiles. Worse yet, Romans typically hated Christians. But Cornelius obeys, the beginning of this breakthrough.

At this same time Peter receives a vision from the Lord where he is instructed to choose an animal to kill and eat. The problem is that the animals presented are both "clean" and "unclean." In the laws given in Leviticus the Israelites were forbidden to eat animals God defined as "unclean." So Peter, a law-abiding Jew, refuses.

The vision concludes with those church-changing words, "Do not call anything impure that God has made clean" (Acts 10:15). While Peter didn't know the exact application of this vision when Cornelius's men arrive in Joppa, Peter accepts their request.

Breakthrough!

God is making Cornelius, a Roman Gentile, clean. Peter's willingness to stay in Cornelius's home broke every Jewish social restriction of the time. New Christians were still trying to understand how to interpret Christ's words that He came to fulfill the law and not to abolish it (Matt. 5:17). What did this mean for their understanding of religious laws and customs? Could they now eat meats that had for generations been unclean? Could a Christian Jew dine and stay with a Christian Gentile?

This social and cultural breakthrough changed everything! But God began this breakthrough by breaking Cornelius and Peter first. Cornelius could have said no. He would have been right to assume that this mission for his men would be a colossal waste of time and money. But God broke though Cornelius's pride and invited this soon-to-be follower into deeper waters of trust.

God broke through Peter's reservations and religious DNA to invite this Spirit-filled spokesperson to take the gospel to outcasts who were now welcomed in. This is monumental, but let me tell you that this was not widely celebrated or accepted at first. (A helpful, but secondary principle of this passage of Scripture.)

Cornelius and Peter's small acts of brokenness—for them, the breaking of their cultural pride—paved the way for our restoration. Thousands of years and millions of ripples later, we are blessed by their "yes." Brokenness is the bridge that we cross toward transformation.

If we passionately pursue brokenness and transformation, we will find the freedom that comes from living confident and unashamed. We will embrace the opportunity to share both our spiritual successes and struggles all for the glorious purpose of making much of Jesus.

This leads us to our final category of transparency: *mature transparency.* This kind of tell-all deals with all of the broken places but also takes time to highlight the beauty that comes from that brokenness. This is the stained-glass window effect. Mature transparency gives God the glory for what He may be doing or has done. You see, mature transparency hasn't always arrived on the other side of brokenness. I've been deeply, deeply challenged by women who have shared from a place of struggle. But their brokenness wasn't because they doubted God's goodness or provision. No. They could look back at what He had done in the past and fix their faith on what He might do again in their future. They were confident in His character no matter their circumstances. Mature transparency isn't always the finished process.

Sick of Me

But sometimes that kind of transparency, where we can share the end of the story, is deeply transformational too. It's a powerful vision-caster for those of us still in the hard area between hope and healing.

Can I take just a bit of a detour here and say something kind of difficult? I've noticed a trend lately where younger Christians look down on the older women and their more saccharine stories of faith and Christian experience. We don't like the doilies, lace, and tidy wisdom of our senior saints. We give it the spiritual side-eye. As though because the end is lovely, it must not be sincere, raw, or real. For those faithful women who have planned the women's brunches, organized the Bible study breakfasts, or sent the prayer cards, I'm so sorry. We owed you more appreciation. You deserved better from us.

Young, in-the-trenches Christians, let's not look down on their feel-good stories. Most of these women have fought through heartache and disappointment for their faith. The moments didn't feel good I'm sure, but they chose not to wallow or make much of their own tragedies or heartache. While it may be a generational generality, those gray-haired beauties were not quite so quick to lament what was hard in their lives. They took the good and the bad and soldiered on. Rather than looking on them with condescension, we would do better to learn from their quiet strength and optimism. We look at the end of their stories, all rainbows and sunshine and assume it must be fake. But maybe, just maybe, she chose the rainbow despite the rain. That doesn't make her story less valuable. In fact, most of us could learn a thing or two from her.

Side bar over. Here's my point. Premature transparency hints at a deeper spiritual issue. And while all of us may slip into

158

it from time to time, we don't want to stay stuck there. Immature transparency pretends to be something we are not. Both will barter contrived confession to get either the approval of others or the appearance of holiness. Mature transparency—real, genuine, non-manipulative transparency—believes that while we may struggle we also experience the Christ-exalting high of seeing what the Holy Spirit does with a bunch of broken women. It's a stunning both/and—broken *and* beautiful.

Women who live confident and unashamed celebrate Christ, share selflessly, and build one another up. We don't let her successes make us feel like failures. We use it as the best kind of accountability, and thank God that there are women in our lives who have strengths that compensate for our weaknesses.

We can't just want the broken, beaten-up side of transparency. That's immature. Legit transparency welcomes it all. Success and failure. Hardship and hope. We get it all. And the church is better for it.

Transparency is good. It's beneficial. But for sure it isn't the endgame. *Transformation* is. *Sanctification* is.

Maybe all of this is brand-new to you. Perhaps as we've walked through these categories you've seen yourself and maybe some of your girlfriends. I bet you can think back to coffee shop conversations, small group, or Sunday school confessions. And you know, like I do, that you need to rethink your transparency strategy. Maybe you're realizing along with me that a lot of our real and raw moments are far, far too much about us. Friend, this has been a startling and hard, hard lesson for me. So I spent some time trying to crystallize the difference between transparency and transformation because I don't want to get stuck in the transparency trap. See if this resonates with you.

Sick of Me

Transparency wants to be seen for who I am.
Mature transparency encourages me to be who
God wants me to be.

Transparency longs to see the broken and
vulnerable.
Mature transparency celebrates what God does
with broken things.

Transparency looks for what's wrong in others
to help me feel better about myself.
Mature transparency looks for how I can be an
accountability partner to help others.

Transparency exclusively shares from a position of struggle.
Mature transparency shares from a position of
submission.

Transparency looks for others to validate us.
Mature transparency looks for what God says
about us and how He's changing us.

Transparency looks for others to affirm us.
Mature transparency wants God to affirm His
presence with us.

Transparency is convinced this is how I'll
always be.

Mature transparency believes that God can
change me.

I don't know about you, but I don't want to get caught in
the trap of immature or premature transparency. I want to be
a woman who pushes past my own pride, insecurities, and pain
to get at the gospel goal of sanctification. Let's spend some time
with a few of these comparisons to help us build a list of must-
dos as we do our part in the pursuit of sanctification.

Going to God First

There's a really, really important first principle that we need
to address when it comes to doing our part in transparency
and sanctification. It presumes that before I confess to others, I
have actually been convicted by the Lord. Immature transparency skips this step, blurting out our woes or struggles though
we're not actually experiencing a burden from God about them.
Premature transparency feels the sting of conviction, but forgets
that real repentance involves not just confession, but change.
But here's the point, it's not enough that God already knows the
truth about us. We need to let *Him* address our sin. We confess
because God is up to something in us and asking us to deal
with it, not because we want to be seen as real or relevant or
understood. Confessing or "being transparent" should always be
initiated by God. It's not fun or pretty, but it's the biblical model.

Why do we need to let God deal with sin? Why do we need
to be confronted by it? Confession keeps us humble. You see if

we are lucky enough to string together a few spiritual successes, we can often forget just how desperately we need the Lord. And one of the ways God often snatches us back from this kind of complacency is through hardship. As painful as confession may be, it's easier than the alternative. (More on that in a bit.)

Scripture is full of stories of people who forgot just how broken they are. People who became overly confident and reckless. Check out just one instance.

Numbers 20:12 says, "But the LORD said to Moses and Aaron, 'Because you did not trust in me enough to honor me as holy in the sight of the Israelites, you will not bring this community into the land I give them.'"

Moses has come a long way from fearful shepherd to faithful leader. The years spent in Midian tending the flock of his father-in-law must have been good preparation for shepherding the whiny, stubborn Israelites. Moses trusts God's provision even as the people constantly complain and doubt.

How quickly faith can falter.

Once again, the Israelites are complaining, this time about a lack of water. In Exodus 17 they voiced the same complaint. Then, God instructed Moses to strike the rock in front of the people. Now, God tells Moses to take his staff and go out, speak to the rock, and water for the people will flow.

Moses *kind of* obeys. He gets it *almost* right. He stops shy of full obedience. Let's learn from Moses' example two important faith principles:

God never excuses sin.

Partial obedience is disobedience.

First, Moses and Aaron walk out in front of the people and ask, "Listen, you rebels, must we bring you water out of this rock?" (Num. 20:10). Now, he's totally right about the "rebels" part. But it's not Moses and Aaron that bring water from the rock. Right from the beginning, we see the condition of Moses' heart; pride has taken root. Perhaps it's frustration. Perhaps it's exhaustion. Why does Moses act so out of character? We don't know. What we know for sure is that Moses and Aaron take credit for God's miraculous provision. No matter the motive, God does not excuse sin.

Second, Moses strikes the rock rather than speaking to it. And just to make sure we recognize the willful neglect of God's command, the Bible records that Moses struck the rock twice. This may seem like a small thing, but again, God does not excuse sin, and partial obedience is disobedience.

For this offense God tells Moses that neither he nor Aaron will enter the Promised Land. All this time spent shepherding these people, listening to their complaints, interceding for them before the Lord and their sin will keep them from the Promised Land. Does this seem terribly harsh to you? I mean, poor Moses and Aaron.

> God never excuses sin, and partial obedience is disobedience.

And there's my problem. I think there are some sins that aren't that big of a deal, but God never excuses sin. When He judges, He judges rightly.

God says it was their lack of trust and refusal to honor Him. Are we guilty of trying to hijack God's glory for ourselves? Do we want to control a situation rather trusting God's process? And finally, do we wonder why God doesn't just look the other way when we offend Him or give us a pass when our pride trumps our faith? God never excuses sin, and partial obedience is disobedience.

Transparency with others ought to happen only after transparency with the Lord. Confessing to others will never take the place of confessing to Him.

Conviction versus Condemnation

Confession is important. This is where God makes us aware of the places in us that keep us from growing. Confession aligns our hearts with His and keeps us humble. Confession reminds us that sin is serious and that grace isn't cheap. Jesus paid for our sins, each and every one of them. Though it's not fun, confession is for sure preferable over condemnation, a place where I often live instead. Here we see the second principle we need to keep in mind when it comes to pursuing true transparency and sanctification: we confess out of conviction, not condemnation.

Jesus talks about conviction and condemnation in John 16. In this passage, He prepares the disciples for His departure and tells them of the promise, power, and presence of the Holy Spirit. John 16:8–11 says, "When he comes, he will prove the world to be in the wrong about sin and righteousness and judgment: about sin, because people do not believe in me; about righteousness, because I am going to the Father, where you can see me no longer; and about judgment, because the prince of this world now stands condemned."

Conviction and condemnation are similar in that they both reveal that we've missed a mark. Conviction, though, comes from the Holy Spirit and addresses our sin and points us to Christ. Condemnation is a weapon of the devil, and by nature, the opposite of conviction. The devil never points us to Christ. No, he'd much rather keep us focused on ourselves. His goal in condemnation is to get us so depressed and frustrated that we give up, or so proud that we double down and try harder in our own self-effort. Condemnation will lead us to legalism or complacency, because either way, we're never enough.

Oh, but when the Holy Spirit convicts, He points out our sin and then points us to the source of our righteousness—Jesus. Conviction will always move us toward the cross where Jesus will empower us to do what we cannot do on our own. Conviction never leaves us stuck in sin, but always moves us toward change.

While our circumstances are what God uses in the process of change and sanctification, once we are convicted by the Holy Spirit, we pursue that change through obedience and faith. With the context that God calls His people to be separate and that separate is hard, we shouldn't be surprised that obedience to what God calls us to will be difficult as well. But that's not the message that we often hear circulated on Facebook or Instagram, right?

This leads us to our next principle when it comes to our pursuit of the sanctification process: obedience always brings blessing. I've heard that message preached, but Exodus 2 teaches us we must be very careful what we expect for our obedience and what we define as a blessing.

Fearing the growth and potential power of the Hebrew slave nation, Pharaoh orders that all baby boys be murdered.

Jochebed, Moses' biological mother, hides her son and then entrusts his life to the protection of God alone. It is a bold, faith-filled move. But the results are a mixed bag of blessings. We can learn a few important lessons from her example.

First, we see that blessings on this side of eternity are temporary.

Jochebed receives the blessing of a healthy baby boy that she would hold, but that blessing is brief. When she realizes she can't keep him hidden any longer, she puts him in a basket and places the basket in among the reeds of the Nile. The word for "basket" here is the same word used to describe Noah's ark. This basket would also be a picture of God's great grace and protection.

Next, we learn that obedience positions us to see God work in spectacular ways.

Jochebed trusts her baby of blessing to the careful watch of her good God. God did not disappoint. He directed the Egyptian princess to come, find the baby, and rescue him. Watching this unfold from a distance, Moses' sister, Miriam, offers to find a Hebrew woman to nurse the baby.

Jochebed would be given the privilege of nursing and raising her son likely for three years! But she would return him to Pharoah's daughter, return him to the careful watch of the God who saw and blessed her faith. As Moses grew, so did Jochebed's faith.

Next, we see that obedience does not always remove our difficulties.

Let's not forget an important detail—she still had to give her baby boy up, again! She had received the sweet, but temporary blessing of caring for her son. But the greater blessing was a faith that knew her son was safest in the hands of her God. This is why we must be careful not to barter our obedience for God's blessings. Our blessing may be things we cannot see.

Over the landscape of this entire story, we can conclude that obedience builds our faith.

Our greatest blessings and most precious rewards are the eternal ones. I want God to grow my faith, refine my character, and chisel away my selfishness. Those treasures won't always feel like blessings. I'd like to be the kind of person who trusts God to give and define my blessings. I'd rather be changed for eternity than comforted temporarily.

Conviction reminds us that the power to change doesn't depend on us, but calls us to respond in faith and obedience. Condemnation has us focused on self. We all know that's a problem because believers are called to be selfless. The intent is that we ought to think less of our needs and more to the needs of others. This is a virtue, indeed.

The Right Way to Look at Ourselves

But can we take this ideal too far? What happens when we don't think of ourselves at all? What would it look like if we never examined our hearts, attitudes, and motives? What if we never address the selfish parts of our "self"? When it comes to transparency and Christ-centered community, it's not that we never take a look at ourselves or need another to take a look at us. The goal is for us to care about the right person who is doing the looking. Rather than focusing on what others think of us, we sometimes need to think about what *Jesus* thinks of us.

In 1 Corinthians 11, Paul gives us a final principle when it comes to our pursuit of transparency and sanctification: focus on yourself, yes, but in the right way. In this passage, Paul is addressing a dysfunction within the church at Corinth. First Corinthians 11:27–28 says, "So then, whoever eats the bread or drinks the cup of the Lord in an unworthy manner will be guilty of sinning against the body and blood of the Lord. Everyone ought to examine themselves before they eat of the bread and drink from the cup."

In casually observing the Lord's Supper, celebrating Jesus' last meal and sacrificial death on the cross, they were alienating members of the church. This holy sacrament, meant to bring unity to the body, was instead causing division.

In Roman meals, it was not uncommon for guests to be seated and served food according to their social status. Wealthier guests were served first and given the best food with ample supply. Those with humbler means were served last and given what was left, if anything. Apparently, this cultural norm had trickled into the church.

So, Paul challenges the members of the church to examine themselves using the principles he has taught in earlier portions of the letter. While they may be free to eat and drink, they must not use their liberty to harm their brother or sister. Our liberty is not just for our good; it is primarily for God's glory. He is glorified when we treat others with honor, dignity, and respect no matter their social or economic status. In this regard Paul certainly wanted them to be more selfless—to stop thinking of themselves so much, and think of God and others.

That isn't Paul's only issue with the Corinthians. Also problematic was that believers were celebrating "the Lord's Supper" as a common meal. Paul explains that this is not the intention. All meals that believers celebrate together are not the same as the holy sacrament of the Lord's Supper. It is sacred, special, and intended to focus our hearts on the sacrificial work of Jesus on our behalf. In other words, it's not the same thing as a "covered dish." (All my Southern church girls know what I'm talking about.)

Paul says that in preparation of this meal, though they were thinking of themselves too much in some ways, these believers were also simultaneously guilty of not examining themselves enough! The Corinthian believers were attending to the Lord's Supper without proper self-assessment and preparation. Their lack of attention wasn't just irresponsible or irreverent; Paul calls it a sin against the body and blood of Jesus. Selfless isn't the same as self-ignorant.

Healthy biblical community requires self-reflection. We think of ourselves—our unconfessed sins, our prideful disagreements, or our unrepentant attitudes (just to name a few). Paul's word "examine" means to scrutinize, deem worthy, or test as genuine. This kind of self-examination isn't the same thing as being selfish or self-absorbed; in fact, it helps make us ready to live well with one another.

Think of the impact in our local churches if, using Paul's example, we thought about ourselves a little bit more? What if we looked often at our hearts, our motives, and our failures. Then what if we took those to the cross and asked Jesus to heal and help us? What if we could then celebrate that the gospel actually works?

What if we were the kind of women who felt free to be ourselves and bring God glory no matter the circumstance? Doesn't that sound so liberating? That feels like a life that is confident and unashamed.

Transformed

If there is a common thread among women of my generation and younger, it seems that many want to be part of something, to feel connected to a community, a movement, something that is bigger than themselves. I can't say I'm that different. I want my life to make an impact. I'd like to think that I'm a part of God's plan to truly change my family, my community, and my corner of the world for the kingdom. But when I think about what that might look like, rarely do I consider my own personal holiness. When I do consider it, I rarely do more than give it a passing thought. I'll talk about it but not do much about it.

And yes, it's made me sick. Sick of me. But what if we—you and me—decided here and now to change? As in actually change. Because confession is easy. Change is hard. But for a generation of women who want to be a part of something, let's be a part of that. Let's be the generation of women who are actually transformed by the power of the gospel.

Better yet, what if we were the kind of women who lived the power of the gospel and proudly proclaimed its effectiveness?

The power to change the kingdom isn't built by organizations or movements. Kingdom change happens in one devoted heart at a time.

We want to live a life of authentic holiness that demonstrates the power of God to take broken women and make them beautiful. And in the daily living of that, my hope, is that we'd be described as women who are confident and unashamed. We are confident in the promise of Christ to cover our past. We are confident in the presence of Christ to sustain us. We are confident in the power of Christ to transform us.

And can you imagine what it might look like to live in community together unashamed to confess our failures and unashamed to celebrate our successes? I'd love to resist the trap of confessing my failures just to keep others from seeing them first. It's exhausting to hold up the pretense of transparency just so others will think I'm committed to change, when really, I just want to keep living like I am.

I'd love to live the authentic reality of messy but maturing life of a Christ-follower. I'd love to see sanctification do the work it was always meant to do: heal us all of our "me" sickness.

But most of my life doesn't look like that. Even now, when I know some helpful things to do and look for, I'm scared I'll fall back into my old patterns. If there is anything consistent in my life, it's the regular pattern of strong starts and too-quick stops. I am not a finisher. I have seen genuine, progressive change in my walk with Jesus, but it's been scarce.

I so want this season of life to be different. But it will take work because God calls His people to be separate. Separate is hard. Hard is good. But God, oh friend, He is best. This won't be celebrated or popular. Because if we're honest, most Christians don't really want to be reminded that Jesus actually expects us to live holy, set apart lives.

Why do I know this? Because more times than I'd like to admit, I've been that Christian—comfortable and happy to confess, but not all that committed to change. I like being happy.

Holy? Well, I'd like to say I'm working on that. But it will change my old patterns, habits, and preferences.

It's not going to feel right for quite a while. But do we really want to feel quite right here?

When you read the news or look at the circumstances of your life, does it seem like this world has gone crazy? While many of us may find that state of our culture upsetting, following Jesus means we see the choices before us and the circumstances around us in completely different ways. In that sense, the culture around us should feel off or kind of crazy to us.

Right Living in an Upside-Down World

In Luke 6, we see a collection of teachings and interactions between Jesus, His disciples, and the religious leaders. There is a thread of consistency between the stories. Jesus was teaching those around Him how to both think and live differently than the norm, counterintuitively and counterculturally. What He teaches doesn't make sense, and it doesn't fit the culture. Luke 6:32–33 says, "If you love those who love you, what credit is that to you? Even sinners love those who love them. And if you do good to those who are good to you, what credit is that to you? Even sinners do that."

You see, in Luke's day, Jesus spent as much time correcting wrong religious thinking as anything else. Biblical thinking is more than moral behavior modification. It's more than church lingo. It's right living in an upside-down world. And Jesus' teaching is that this kind of living ought to touch every aspect of our lives.

Here's a sampling of Jesus' teachings:

> When questioned by the religious leaders as to why He would heal on the Sabbath, Jesus says regardless of religious convention (which is different than religious conviction) it is better to heal and serve than ignore or condemn. Religious leaders said, "Put people off and follow protocol." That had become the cultural norm. Jesus' authority as Lord of the Sabbath frees His people to follow His authority, not tradition. Jesus was putting people above protocol and paradigms. Think about how living like this would truly change our culture.[4]

When teaching how to love others, Jesus says culture expects us to love those who love us back. "Normal" says we lend to those who can and will pay us back. Jesus wants His followers to defy cultural expectations and extend lavish love and grace even on their enemies and those powerless to benefit us. Think about how treating others like this would radically impact our culture.

To live counter to the culture rarely feels good. These notions were radical then and now. To read and understand what Jesus asks of us is entirely different than actually doing it. But this is the radical part of radical living—doing what Jesus calls us to do, not just thinking about it (Luke 6:46–49). This kind of living is really the call of the gospel. Jesus invites us to change the world around us with a radical way of living and loving. Our world could use a heavy dose of this kind of Jesus-culture.

But I'd like to think that being transformed by the gospel won't just change us but will also by extension change those around us. Isn't that the goal of community? Yes. I think it is.

Now here's the hard part. The part that must be said because, well, this book makes a big deal about transparency. We may want to believe the best about people, and I think that's a virtue. But I also think we should prepare ourselves that not everyone will celebrate this change. And that's why we will desperately, desperately need each other.

The church.

The collection of God's people is the place where we can cheer each other on and challenge one another to pursue Christ. It's the group of people who will hold our hand when the call to be separate is unbearably hard. You guys, I know she has her problems. I know you know that too. She is far from perfect because, let's be honest, you and I are far from perfect. But together, as we stay committed to the process and pursuit of sanctification, we can be rescued from ourselves, living collectively the kind of truly transformed lives that change us and the world.

That sounds good, right? But that change, any change really, begins with the decision to leave something that *wasn't good* in pursuit of something *better*. Or maybe sometimes it's the commitment to leave something that *was good* in the pursuit of something, or Someone that is *best*. Either way, it's the commitment to change. For me, that began with the awareness that I was just plain sick of myself. I was sick of being stuck. I was talking about all the things. I was transparent, but I wasn't being transformed.

Oh friend, I'd never want to dump all my hang-ups on you. Maybe you've read along thinking, *How sad for her. She's a train wreck.* I'd be okay with that. Really. Because goodness gracious, it's true from time to time. But I don't know that we get to the end, as we journey through the junk, of a book that doesn't somehow reflect something true about ourselves. So, I don't want to lay this on you, but if you're here at the end with me, is it fair to say that, maybe, you're kind of sick of you too?

Like me, are you ready to stop chasing happiness and actually pursue holiness? Because I've chased the happy life (all while calling it holy), and friend, I know it's not the endgame. Deep in my soul, it wasn't enough. I was left still wanting more—unsatisfied and longing for Jesus to do more in me than what I had been able to do for myself.

I am committed to let Him work me through the process of holiness. I want to say "yes" to sanctification. Now though, I'm ready. I finally get that it's more than church-going and quiet times. Sanctification isn't only about what I do. No. God wants to mess with who I am. The stuff on the inside. He's got major work to do in me. And He has work to do in you too.

There is a curious tension about that process though. He changes our inside through circumstances on the outside. He works His process by calling us out of what makes us comfortable. We are called to be separate, and that is just plain hard. I've realized that for most of my life I've run away from hard, avoided pain, and ultimately short-circuited the very thing God wanted to use to bring change in my life. I want to be a woman who cooperates with God and embraces the work He's doing to make me more holy. Ultimately, hard is good.

But more than that, I want to be a woman who also pursues the work of holiness in my life. Can you imagine what our lives might look like if we confessed what's broken in us, and then chased the better version not of ourselves, but chased Christ? In the end, that's what it's about. God is best. Life *with* Christ and life *like* Christ is best.

Finally, in all these hard places and growing seasons, we're going to need the support of our people around us. If that's true, what if we learned how to live transparently with those people? What if we were women who were honest in our pursuit of holiness, not happiness? Let's receive the grace for our brokenness and the accountability to be better. Can we live out the tension that we are both simultaneously broken and yet better than we were? Friend, I suspect our churches would explode if we proclaimed that the gospel is good, and that it works. I want to be the crazy woman shouting, "Look what He's doing in me!" Am I terrified that some might judge me? You betcha. But I know, deep in my soul I know, that it's Jesus. Only Jesus. And I don't want to keep hiding the good, albeit sometimes small work He's doing in me, in the name of brokenness and transparency.

Let's do it. You and me. Together. Today. Decide to join God in the process He is already working out in you. Do your part. Be about the pursuit. And see how God will take you from mere confession to actual change, or from transparency into real transformation.

You don't have to live sick of yourself, in the same old place you were before.

The cure for my me-sickness is more and more of Him. It's a prescription I'm ready to take.

Notes

1. Julie Andrews, "Do-Re-Mi." *The Sound of Music,* 45th Anniversary Edition, Sony Legacy, 2010. Audio CD.

2. P. J. Achtemeier, *Harper's Bible Dictionary* (San Francisco, CA: Harper & Row and Society of Biblical Literature, 1985), 1,153.

3. Robert Mounce, *Romans: An Exegetical and Theological Exposition of Holy Scripture* (Nashville, TN: Broadman and Holman, 1995), 131.

4. Whitney Capps, "A Countercultural Church" at https://first5.org/plans/Luke/ff_luke_10/.

Proverbs 31
MINISTRIES

About Our Ministry

If you were inspired by *Sick of Me* and desire to deepen your own personal relationship with Jesus Christ, I encourage you to connect with Proverbs 31 Ministries.

Proverbs 31 Ministries exists to be a trusted friend who will take you by the hand and walk by your side, leading you one step closer to the heart of God through:

Free online daily devotions
First 5 Bible study app
Daily radio program
Books and resources
Online Bible Studies
COMPEL Writers Training:
www.CompelTraining.com

To learn more about Proverbs 31 Ministries call 877-731-4663 or visit www.Proverbs31.org.

Proverbs 31 Ministries
630 Team Rd., Suite 100
Matthews, NC 28105
www.Proverbs31.org